PREPARATION FOR ELEVATION:
ASCENSION IN GOD'S KINGDOM

Dennis J. Perkins

Please direct all copyright inquiries to:

Dennis J. Perkins

Dperkins2415@comcast.net

Paperback ISBN:979-889480-407-1

Printed in the United States

DEDICATION

This book is dedicated to my brother Charles (Chuck) L. Perkins. He contended with and endured many of life's tests and trials but also experienced countless victories. The greatest of all victories was his profession of faith in Jesus Christ as his Lord and Savior.

Chuck was a person of excellence. You could see it in anything that he set out to do. When at his best, he never believed in doing anything halfway. He had many interests and took great pride and joy in his work, but in his unique way, he showed an even greater appreciation for the genuine love of family and lasting friendships.

Life is so valuable. We should never take even one moment of any given day for granted. To know the abundant life that Jesus Christ gives brings the most significant essence to the time that we enjoy now and throughout eternity.

May the peace of GOD that passes understanding keep your heart and mind in Christ Jesus. (Philippians 4:7).

Many blessings and much love.

SPECIAL ACKNOWLEDGEMENTS

I want to thank my Father in Heaven, Jesus Christ, and the Holy Spirit for inspiring me and giving me the insights for this book.

Bishop Arthur Knight, you and your beautiful wife, Sister Doris Knight, have served as an extension of GOD'S grace and encouragement for me You helped to re-ignite the fire in me to publish this book. I love and appreciate all that you do for me and others. I pray that GOD will provide all your needs according to His riches in glory, spirit, soul, and body. In Jesus' name. Amen.

Other Acknowledgments

*Those who have consistently been there for me in the best and most difficult times: These acknowledgments are not listed in any particular order.

Apostle-Pastor Juanita Ward

Prophetess Sha'Neika (Neiky) Christian

Drs. Samuel & Shirley Perkins and Family

Dr. Wesley D. Granger

Bertha S. Perkins

Beth M. Townsend

Vern & Faye Perkins and Family

Tina L. Wallace

Apostles Calvin & Vivian Brown and Family

Mrs. Rosemary Perkins

Larry & Evelyn Willis

Joe & Sybla Rule

Vernon & Frances Meeks and Family

Robert & Patricia Perkins and Family

Deborah L. Hunter

LaDonna Marie Cook

Jeremiah Granger

Sharrell Campbell

Keisha Perkins

Timothy Clark

Markus & Sybil Meadows and Family

Pastors Bernard & Lois Johnson

John & Rene Jones and Family

Jeremy & Shani Armon and Family

Erta Faye Logan and Family

Ty & Jessica Bailey and Family

Emery & Trudy Mayoros and Family

Peter & Mary Ellen Ciganovich

Dr. Teresa Smith

Cyrus Webb

Melissa Banks

Frederick & Pauline Rogers

Cynthia Thompson

Thomas & Mary Ward and Family

David Dogan

Arthur Noble

Willie & Kimberly Wynn and Family

Gloria Wynn

Otis Taylor'

James Williams

Charles Grady

Willie & Betty Blackmon

COVER DESIGN

Thank you, Tyler Ferrell, for lending your imagination, artistic gifts, and the anointing on your life to help make this project successful.

Contact Tyler at Tylerdferrell@gmail.com

LITERARY-PUBLISHING CONSULTANT

Thank you, April Metzler. You have been a treasure trove of knowledge throughout this process and helped make it a joyful and rewarding experience.

Contact April at Admin@aprilmetler.com

INTERIOR DESIGN CONSULTANT

Thank you, Sherry Jones. You have generously shared your delightful energy, sound guidance, and wisdom with me, helping me to gain a greater appreciation and respect for the book publishing process.

Contact Sherry at sherry@sherryspeakslife.com

Table of Contents

INTRODUCTION

We are living in rapidly changing times. The changes are far too numerous to count. As the days progress, they are increasingly impactful for societies and nations. There are wars and rumors of wars, numerous predictions of financial crashes, bank failures, pandemics, and racial, cultural, social, and political upheaval everywhere. Whenever you're tempted to look back at how things were a few short years ago, it will never resurrect or relive the more pleasant memories of that time. The changes we have witnessed and continue to experience are much more definitive today than at any other time in our remembrance. We are headed towards the dawn of a new era that will affect us all in many ways. This new era will be filled with the revelation of GOD'S word. GOD'S word is the truth. The word of GOD is more genuine in context and relevant to the world than any written communication ever authored. Men whom the Holy Spirit inspired wrote as they received the guidance to do so.

In John 17:17-19 (NIV), Jesus said in His prayer to His heavenly Father,

Sanctify them by the truth; Your word is truth.

As you have sent Me into the world, I have sent them into it.

For them, I sanctify Myself, that they too may be truly sanctified.

What is widely projected in our media, educational institutions, and some of our pulpits is skillfully crafted to generate predictable reactions. Many of our institutions have struggled to maintain their relevance because they have lost the purity and focus of their purpose. Despite their distinct relationships with the communities, many of our institutions are held captive by the shifting norms and influences that society dictates. So, there should be no surprise that these entities generally provide services from this perspective. It is incredible how the world operates.

We currently exist in what many refer to as the third dimension. The first three dimensions concern our knowledge about reality (descriptive, normative, practical). The fourth and fifth dimensions concern knowing knowledge (critical, dialectical). The sixth dimension integrates the other five dimensions (synthetic) (Springer Link—The Six Dimensions of Philosophy/First Online: 01 January 2014, pp 3-11).

When you begin to tap into the knowledge of GOD, you'll quickly find that it is the highest of all dimensions. There is no other knowledge to compare with what GOD reveals to us by His Holy Spirit. So, regardless of the metaphysical or the natural sciences, there is no higher knowledge than the Lord's. The Lord desires to draw us closer to Him, but that process is activated by faith and our total surrender. There is a high calling in GOD. Yes, He wants us to come into the higher realms, which can only be acquired in His presence. GOD'S Spirit is often imitated but is impossible to duplicate. The spirit realm without GOD is the equivalent of idolatry and witchcraft. Even when people innocently engage in these practices without evil intent, they open themselves up to a world of darkness and deception. They open spiritual portals that release demonic influences that can envelop all that concerns them. It impacts not only those directly involved but also those closest to them. The spirit realm is an authentic world that should never be taken for granted. Remember, GOD is Spirit, and those who worship Him must worship in spirit and truth. (John 4:24). The spirit realm comes under His authority. Even the demons believe and tremble that there is one GOD. (James 2:19). The word of GOD urges us to test, not some, but every spirit to see if it is of Him.

1 John 4:1 ESV says,

Beloved, do not believe every spirit, but test the spirits to see whether they are from GOD, for many false prophets have gone out into the world.

Without the Holy Spirit, we are void of the Lord's guidance. He is the One sent to lead and guide us into all truth. It is puzzling why men do not desire to know or retain anything concerning GOD's knowledge. (Romans 1:28).

Whatever God does is always beneficial to those He loves and to those who exhibit their love for Him by keeping His commandments.

Many institutions are now more emersed in efforts to appease their funding sources instead of serving as an integral lifeline to our communities. Their trust does not abide in GOD but rather in the agencies they receive resources from. They take on a position of compromise that considerably lowers and altogether eliminates any degree of excellence. Because of this, the original stance and true purpose for their existence are lost. They, in turn, operate in survival mode. What do I mean by that? Many people in institutional settings minimally engage themselves in the individual concerns of their customers/clients. They deliver a service without exhibiting any genuine quality of compassion or care. They do just enough to cover their bases to benefit themselves while leaving those served with the feeling of being passed down an assembly line. What are we missing? It is the element of genuine caring and sharing in an atmosphere that values each individual as GOD'S unique creation, made in His image. This is the system that individuals are taught to perpetuate from generation to generation. It is a system designed to take, rather than give, to exploit rather than give others equal consideration while showing mutual respect to everyone with the highest regard. Many people in leadership positions have taken on the institution's attitude and have become an island unto themselves.

The enemy has also typically used established institutions to implement an epidemic of ill-preparedness throughout the populations worldwide. Rather than raising the standard, they promote ideologies that indoctrinate and prevent genuine efforts to present the knowledge without compromise. They must base their services on the simplicity of presenting the truth as a priority. They weaponize the sacredness of their duties and violate those who corporately entrust their families and communities to them. We gradually relinquish our freedoms until we are deeply entangled in a ruthless web of lies. The truth should never be side-stepped, diluted, or misrepresented.

Much of what we see and hear from our most trusted information sources is filled with suggestive forms of programming. These greatly aid in solidifying a created illusion of life that further breeds inadequacy and fear-based perceptions of real life.

We are in an information war composed of words and images. The enemy knows how to use the power of words and images in their seed form to subtly plant them into our souls (through our minds, wills, and emotions). When there is wrongfully intended seeding into the soil of one's heart, it will only produce a harvest of contaminated fruit. Whether the condition of the

14

soil is good or of lesser quality, there will be a change in the soil's original composition. This is what unresolved sin does to the heart of man. Placing good soil over the contaminated soil may work to some degree, but removing the bad soil will be the best remedy to vastly improve the quality of the new growth. We must view this in terms that will challenge us to the point of knowing that we need to change how we have been programmed to process and learn. We have been programmed to think like the crowd, follow the crowd, and be like the crowd. What appears to be foreign to the majority instantly becomes unpopular and unacceptable. Whether the cultural belief system is true or false, anyone viewed as a misfit is duly rejected and isolated from the rest of the crowd. Romans 12:1-2 tells us that we are not to be conformed to the ways of this world, but to be changed or transformed by renewing our minds. We are also told that if anyone is in Jesus Christ, they are considered a new creature. Old things have passed away, and all things are made new. (2 Corinthians 5:17).

We Have All Things In Common – Our True Roots

The devil's mission is always to sway or convince the soul to agree with the alternative to the truth. So, instead of believing the truth, we take the optional route that compliments and supports the lie.

This poses the same spiritual influence that the serpent used to tempt Adam and Eve in the Garden of Eden. He subtly seduced them to disobey GOD'S holy ordinance that served to keep them within the boundaries of His abundant life for them. The Tree of the Knowledge of Good and Evil became the object of focus to lead them to sin.

Genesis 2:16-17 says,

And the Lord GOD commanded the man, saying, Of every tree of the garden thou mayest freely eat:

But of the tree of the knowledge of good and evil, thou shalt not eat of it; for in the day that thou eatest thereof, thou shalt surely die.

In sequence, it was shortly after GOD speaking the above commandment to Adam that He said,

It is not good that the man should be alone. I will make him an help meet for him. (Genesis 2:18 KJV).

As we see in verse 16, GOD commanded man to eat every tree in the garden freely except for one tree, the tree of the knowledge of good and evil. He told Adam that the day that he chose to disobey and eat of it, he would surely die. After Adam received the Lord's commandment, GOD made the woman Eve. GOD revealed to Adam that he and Eve were made one most intimately and deeply, becoming bone of his bone and flesh of his flesh.

So right out of the gate, the devil instituted his devious plan to disrupt, delay, and ultimately destroy the Kingdom of Heaven's original intent. Thus, the devil's race to possess men's souls began. Chaos ensued as Satan, who manifested himself as the serpent, implemented a plan to cheat, connive, steal, kill, and destroy the man and woman's legal spiritual authority. The devil specializes in bringing accusations against GOD'S redeemed and anointed. His methods have not changed since his beginning. Whether we are aware or unaware, He still roams about as a roaring lion, seeking whom he may devour. 1 Peter 5:7-9 NLT warns us in the Spirit of GOD'S love, to stay alerted to the adversary's wicked devices. This is why he is so busy, seeking to upend any advancement that he may view as a threat to gaining a foothold in a strategic place. It can be in friendship, family, marital relationships, and institutional settings, like our jobs, or churches of today.

Give all your worries and cares to GOD, for He cares about you.

Stay alert! Watch out for your great enemy, the devil. He prowls around like a roaring lion, looking for someone to devour.

Stand firm against him, and be strong in your faith. Remember that your family of believers all over the world is going through the same kind of suffering you are.

So, we must:

1. Stay alert and on guard by staying spiritually sensitive and focused on our prayer life. Guard your heart by guarding every entry point of negative influence from environments. We are subject to the world's snares, but the Holy Spirit is our navigator (John 16:13), and He is the only way.

2. Stand firm by first listening and understanding what the word of GOD says on any given matter. When you admit that you have weaknesses, GOD also knows them, and will always keep you in those times of temptation. He gives you a voice to say no, hands that will not touch what is unclean, and the ability to turn and walk away from temptations that lead to sin. The enemy loves to weaken or destroy our testimony. If he can successfully suppress or severely damage our confidence, we're less likely to stand firm. (Hebrews 3:14; Hebrews 10:35).

3. Be strong in your faith. We must always remember that we can never be braggadocious about our level of faith. True faith comes from hearing what GOD'S word is saying to us. Also, we must acknowledge that circumstances will not change the trajectory of what His word is designated to accomplish. We believe by trusting that whatever GOD says is infallible, complete of integrity, and always the truth. Jesus said in John 17:17, Sanctify them by the truth; Your word is truth.

4. Remember that you are never alone in whatever you suffer for the sake of the Kingdom of GOD. We sometimes tend to think that it is exclusive to us when we are being persecuted, tested, and tried. This is never

the case. We must focus on the fact that others are going through similar, even harsher circumstances than ours. Be careful not to be overly troubled to the point of complaining. As you pray, pray for others as well.

The enemy always harbors and expresses extreme hatred for those who have overcome by the blood of the Lamb and the words of their testimony. (Revelation 12:11). This is one of the primary ways of walking in the truth and authority of your heavenly calling. You and I must always maintain our confidence in the fact that He who has established and continues His good work in us is faithful to complete it. (Philippians 1:6).

Our Father in Heaven made man so unique that it even confounded the angels. Both the male and female were considered beautifully and wonderfully made. Unique to any other, man was specifically created to expand and reinforce GOD'S dominion in the earthly realm. Our Creator's plan for man has not ceased. He once and for all redeemed men, women, girls, and boys from the guilt of sin and much more through Jesus Christ, referred to as the second Adam. 1 Corinthians 15:45-47 KJV says,

And so, it is written, the first man, Adam, was made a living soul; the last Adam was made a quickening spirit.

Howbeit that was not first which is spiritual, but that which is natural; and afterward that which is spiritual.

The first man is of the earth, earthy; the second man is the Lord from heaven.

We have been given creative power through the breath of GOD. This breath is not the mere ability to inhale and exhale. The breath of GOD is spiritual, which is above the three-dimensional realm. GOD imparted His own Spirit into man. Therefore, man became spirit also. In the original Hebrew, a living soul can also be interpreted to mean a speaking spirit. This also changes the mindset and image of who we were created to be. Our words have creative power. Therefore, we have been given the authority to create atmospheres with our words.

Jesus Christ said, *"Have faith in GOD." For assuredly I say to you, whoever says to this mountain, "Be removed and be cast into the sea, and does not doubt in his heart, but believes that those things he says will be done, he will have whatever he says.*

Therefore, I say to you, whatever things you ask when you pray, believe that you receive them, and you will have them. (Mark 11:22-24 NKJV).

We are given the power to speak and create through our words. How else would we be able to have dominion without first speaking that dominion into existence? Our words will activate and eventually manifest what we believe. Since we were created in the image of GOD, the attributes given to us are to be used for their purposes. Words have creative power. Proverbs tells us that death and life are in the power of the tongue, and they that love it will eat the fruit thereof. (Proverbs 18:21). GOD is looking for a people who will take up the mantle of truth to walk in His ways. Therefore, we must walk in the authority originally given through grace. (Matthew 10:8; 1 Corinthians 2:12-16).

What GOD has deposited in you and me is far greater than we know, but we are quickly learning about the authority that belongs to us. We must seek and acquire appropriate answers when we find ourselves ignorant. We should not be destroyed by our lack of knowledge. Knowledge must be activated and then applied to be the most impactful. GOD will always have our best interest at heart and does not ever want us to be left out or come up on the short end of His plans.

Psalm 8:4-8 NIV says,

What is man that You are mindful of him,

And the son of man, You visit him?

For You have made him a little lower than the angels,

And You have crowned him with glory and honor.

You have made him dominion over the works of Your hands; You have put all things under his feet.

All sheep and oxen – even the beasts of the field,

The birds of the air and the fish of the sea that pass through the paths of the seas.

Getting Into the Proper Position to Excel

There is one thing that any true believer in Jesus Christ can attest to; it is that the devil is a liar and the father of lies. (John 8:44). There is no truth in him. He first manifested himself as the serpent in the Garden of Eden. He highlighted what was forbidden to the eyes of the woman, whose name was Eve. In the Book of Genesis, GOD spoke directly to Adam about the forbidden tree. Eve was not present at that time. Therefore, GOD gave direct responsibility to Adam. Genesis 2:15-18 NKJV says,

Then the Lord GOD took the man and put him in the garden of Eden to tend and keep it, entrusting him with this sacred duty.

And the Lord GOD commanded the man, saying, "Of every tree of the garden you may freely eat; but of the tree of the knowledge of good and evil you shall not eat, for the day that you of it you shall surely die.

In Genesis 2:21-25, GOD performed a supernatural surgery upon Adam by taking one of his ribs and from it, made a woman, then the Lord brought her to the man. The point I am making is that the woman was not present when the Lord forbade Adam from eating the fruit of the tree of the knowledge of good and evil. GOD spoke directly to the man. Adam was, therefore, entrusted to carry out the word the Lord gave faithfully. Your willingness to obey whatever GOD is speaking through the written (logos) or the revelation (Rhema), the word of truth, reinforces and establishes GOD'S righteousness on the earth. This was one of the reasons that the serpent approached the woman. Some think GOD does not speak directly to men anymore, as He has done in the past. That is not so. Men can hear and converse with GOD just as the first man.

As the interaction continued between the woman and the deceptive serpent, Eve soon succumbed to his wily, enticing words. Adam was nearby, witnessing the dialogue between the serpent and the woman. The serpent intended to go after the man's authority and position with the Lord. The man was the gatekeeper of the Garden of Eden, charged with keeping and obeying GOD'S word. It was not that Eve bore no responsibility in this matter. The serpent, however, showed his hand, deceitfully gaining illegal access to the most holy affairs of the first family. No one asked for his input, but the serpent persisted in his efforts to discredit what GOD commanded and label Him as a liar. The serpent planted the seeds of doubt and distrust in Eve first, then used her to get Adam off of his post as the gatekeeper of the garden and away from their sacred relationship with GOD. So, the serpent did not enter through the true gatekeeper but sneakily gained access through the woman. This disobedience led to the first family's expulsion from the Garden of Eden, a stark reminder of the consequences of disobedience.

Look at John 10:1 NLT; it says,

I tell you the truth, anyone who sneaks over the wall of a sheepfold rather than going through the gate, must surely be a thief and robber.

But the one who enters through the gate is the shepherd of the sheep.

The gatekeeper opens the gate for him, and the sheep recognizes his voice and come to him. He calls his own sheep by name, and calls them out.

GOD entrusted Adam with the keys to the Garden of Eden. When He commanded the man not to eat of the tree of the knowledge of good and evil, GOD knew that the man and woman were curious beings and would be tempted by the serpent.

This reminded me of when, as a growing boy, my parents would entrust me with specific tasks. I knew I might forget something if I stopped somewhere along the way before completing every aspect of the assignment. If I returned home without completing that task, I was disciplined and told to turn around, finish, and do it right. I had not yet matured enough to become fully accountable, but I thank GOD that they kept giving me opportunities to learn, grow, and honor my responsibilities. As time moved on, their trust and my level of responsibility increased.

The Lord gave Adam and Eve such a test when he placed them in the garden and gave them specific instructions to carry out. Adam became distracted by the outside interferences caused by the serpent's seduction and influence on Eve. He convinced them to exhibit independence from GOD. So, they chose the alternative, believing that there would be no consequence of death. The enemy's plot was devious. He knew that if he engaged the woman, it would bring separation from GOD and arouse distrust in one another. This is how the same spirit of division is allowed to enter our lives.

So, the enemy avoided going through the gatekeeper and went through the side door, representing Adams' side. The rib extracted from the man was what Eve was made from. The rib area was the most vulnerable place for the devil to access. Rather than Adam stepping into his proper position to aggressively defend GOD'S word and the woman, he allowed

Eve to converse with the deceptive serpent. She was distracted from her proper role and left her spiritual position at Adam's side. They did not work together. Two are always better, and much stronger than one who stands alone. They both erred in their response to the serpent's proposal. There was no unity or agreement between the man and the woman. Their position of oneness became fragmented by their yielding to temptation.

Can two walk together except they be agreed? (Amos 3:3).

The enemy plans always to divide us. He sees any unity as a sworn adversary. He hates unity in any form that it takes, especially if it is of GOD. When elevated in the Kingdom of GOD, look for onslaughts of plots and schemes that cause division through strife, confusion, competition, jealousy, and the like. So many allow themselves to be possessed by this spirit of division. They will enable the enemy to subvert them in their ability to make righteous judgments. He uses gas-lighting methods to promote false conclusions as the truth. We need to learn to trust the Lord wholeheartedly and not lean on our understanding of the world's workings. We have been systematically taught how to, when, and why of the rationale on which we base our decisions. We do so without being awakened to the fact that we are operating under a mechanism of control.

As referred to earlier, marriage is an earthly representation of Jesus Christ and the body of believers in Him. It, too, represents the highest form of godly unity in the earthly realm. The enemy cannot understand the ways of the Most High GOD, so he openly detests the divine order of oneness in the Lord. If he showed any regard for order, he would have approached the man first in the garden rather than the woman. He dishonors proper, ordained headship, especially regarding covenant relationships.

1 Corinthians 11:3 says,

But I want you to know that the head of every man is Christ, the head of the woman (wife) is man (the husband), and the head of Christ is GOD.

When you walk in agreement with the Lord, the enemy will find it difficult, on his part, to launch an attack upon you without any successful results. So, he makes attacks that cause distractions and confusion through other people and situations that may directly or indirectly impact you. The spirit of the devil is wired to bring opposition to GOD'S plans and purposes. He can only pay the wages of sin (disobedience), with death as the consequence. When sin continuously goes unchecked, it will undoubtedly lead to spiritual death. The soul's salvation only comes through accepting Jesus Christ as the risen Son of GOD, seated at the right hand of GOD'S throne of majesty.

John 10:10 NIV says,

The thief does not come except to steal and to kill and to destroy. I have come that they may have life and have it more abundantly.

The enemy highly envies the capacity in which GOD demonstrates His love towards us. Remember that John 3:16 tells us how GOD so loved the world that He gave His only begotten Son, that whosoever believes in Him would not perish, but will have everlasting life. The devil cannot comprehend the unmerited favor GOD so graciously and freely gives those who receive Him. He was too cowardly to confront the man, so he chose what was determined to be the way of less resistance. What way was that? It was through the woman, Eve. The serpent initiated the temptation by insinuating that GOD had ulterior motives and was untrustworthy. The serpent insinuated that the Lord lied when He said, "For the day that you eat of the tree, you will surely die." The serpent indicated to her that they would not surely die but would become like GOD. This false assurance was short-lived because it led to one single act of disobedience.

Adam and Eve turned their focus away from the very thing that GOD commanded them not to do. Their original focus became diverted from what the Lord commanded them to do to the serpent's lying perspective. Self-appeasement was initiated through the lust of the eyes; the need to eat of the tree became more prevalent than their willingness to obey the word of life. The two disbelieved the integrity of GOD'S word that was initially spoken to Adam. They were also introduced to the enticement of pride when they believed their eyes would be opened and they would be as GOD, knowing good and evil. So, as the woman continued to look (visual image), she was further enticed to see that the fruit was good for consumption. Nothing withheld her from tasting and offering the same to her husband, Adam, who knew well what GOD had commanded them not to do. They conspired with the serpent to rebel against the Word of the Lord. Upon doing so, they died spiritually and set a precedent for all men to succumb to natural death. Yes, their eyes were opened to a new way of seeing, believing, and independently doing things. This was not the way that GOD intended. They suddenly saw themselves naked and immediately sowed fig leaves together to cover up their shame from being fully exposed. Before this, they had no shame in their nakedness. They once had strong confidence in their relationship with their Holy and Righteous Creator. That depth of relationship was quickly stolen from them. They paid the penalty, which again was spiritual death and separation from GOD. This is what sin does. It robs us of our GOD given identity in exchange for the counterfeit image of the deceiver, who lives in the realm of darkness that is shrouded in lies. The ramifications of this single act were intended to have a devastating and permanent impact on man's eternity, but GOD had an answer. He had a plan of redemption already set in place to save all men (male and female) for eternity.

Embracing the Right Plan

Embracing GOD'S plan has no possibility of failure. It is designed to bring us into our true inheritance. This is what the enemy so desperately wants to keep us away from acknowledging. Proper acknowledgment can be more potent than anything the devil attempts to bring our way. We are in this world, but this doesn't mean we should agree with whatever happens. In Jesus Christ, you are salt and light. You are created to bring heaven's seasoning and enlightenment to this world. Isaiah 60:3 NLT says that all nations will come to your light; mighty kings will come to your radiance. Living boldly in your inheritance in Jesus Christ gives you the confidence to possess what GOD has already prepared for you.

In Him (Jesus Christ) also we have obtained an inheritance, being predestined according to the purpose of Him who works all things according to the counsel of His will that we who first trusted in Christ should be to the praise of His glory.

In Him you also trusted after you heard the word of truth, the gospel of your salvation, in whom also having believed, you were sealed with the Holy Spirit of promise,

who is the guarantee of our inheritance until the redemption of the purchased possession, to the praise of His glory. (Ephesians 1:11-16).

This is why the enemy fights so hard to suppress valuable gifts. Most of the time, we place limitations on ourselves. We can have a lower opinion of ourselves or be overly self-conscious. Sometimes, those in leadership roles tend to allow themselves to be used by the enemy to minimize the use of our gifts and discourage us. When we come into the reality of our calling, it becomes highly threatening to the realm of darkness. This is why the devil uses various tactics to subdue us. In leadership positions, people can deny, misuse, or even misposition us, making it difficult to function properly in our GOD-ordained roles. Over the past few years, we have seen an epidemic of self-appointed apostles and prophets in the church. Many are denied the ability to utilize their gifts in the local churches. Thus, many of them operate outside of the oversight of spiritual authority that the Lord genuinely ordains.

Your Time Has Come

You were born for such a time as this. It doesn't matter that you may feel out of place or are not making a difference. GOD has allotted you time to make your own unique, specific contribution. Your time is not in the great by and by, but it is right now. GOD has chosen and activated you into times and situations that you'd never choose for yourself. You have an assignment to fulfill, and that is never a small thing with GOD. He wants and needs your agreement for the anointing that abides within to be stirred and fully utilized to fulfill His purposes.

Never take anything for granted. Always be alert. Know and understand that sin is always encamped at the door. Therefore, we should never rest on our laurels, by taking our salvation for granted. None of us are exempt from encountering various kinds of trials and temptations that lead to opportunities to engage in sinful acts.

1 John 1:8 NLT says,

If we claim we have no sin, we are only fooling ourselves and not living in the truth.

But if we confess our sins to Him, He is faithful and just to forgive us our sins and to cleanse us from all wickedness.

If we claim we have not sinned, we are calling GOD a liar and showing that His word has no place in our hearts.

Genesis 4:1-7 NLT details how sin found its way into the second generation of man through Cain, who committed the sin of murder that was rooted in the wickedness that he harbored in his heart against his brother, Abel. This act is precipitated from seeds of envy, jealousy, and uncontrollable anger that were previously planted in the heart of Cain. The seeds were given a prolonged time to germinate until they sprouted from the contaminated soil of that man's heart.

Genesis 4:1-7 NLT says,

Now Adam had sexual relations with his wife, Eve and she became pregnant. When she gave birth to Cain, she said, "With the Lord's help, I have produced a man!"

Later, she gave birth to his brother Abel. When they grew up, Abel became a shepherd, while Cain cultivated the ground.

When it was time for the harvest, Cain presented some of his crops as a gift to the Lord.

Abel also brought a gift- the best portions of the first-born lambs from his flock. The Lord accepted Abel and his gift.

But He did not accept Cain and his gift. This made Cain very angry, and he looked dejected.

"Why are you so angry?" the Lord asked Cain. Why do you look so dejected? You will be accepted if you do what is right. But if you refuse to do what is right, then watch out! Sin is crouching at the door, eager to control you. But you must subdue it and be its master. Genesis 4:1-7 NLT.

Therefore, two opposing orders were expressed through Cain and Abel. Good and evil can never work in harmony with each other. One must always overshadow the other. When we refuse to do what is right, then sin will gain legal entry through the door. Whenever GOD is disobeyed, we lose whatever

34

protection is provided to us as opposed to when we obey the Lord. How does this now apply to us? Every word of GOD is for our benefit. Sin never imposes itself upon us without our succumbing to it. Remember, GOD will never allow you or me to be tempted beyond our ability. He will provide a way of escape so that we can endure it. (1 Corinthians 10:13). The war between good and evil will continue until Jesus Christ returns. In the meantime, we must continue to fight the good fight of faith, taking hold of the eternal life that we are called when we make the good confession in the presence of many witnesses. (1 Timothy 6:12). We must create an environment where good overcomes evil every time.

Light Always Wins Over Darkness

Since the beginning, the devil has made attempts to steal the authority that was inherently given to man by creating pathways to sin. The commission of sin leads to spiritual death. When anyone is caught up in the web of sin, continuing in it will disqualify them from experiencing elevation within the Kingdom of GOD. Often, a person can be anointed to serve in a particular capacity while still participating in the throes of sinful acts. We may ask then, why would GOD allow this to happen? The case can be made here that the gifts and callings of GOD are without repentance; they are irrevocable. (Romans 11:29). A gift or calling cannot be earned but is the result of grace given by GOD. Gifts do not belong to the bearer, to use at their discretion, but instead are for those who need what they provide. Many mighty men and women of GOD can quickly become deceived by this, thinking that if their gift continues to function, GOD will be pleased with them and have overlooked their continual indiscretions. This is total deception and one of the many reasons we see so many ministers and ministries of the Gospel of Jesus Christ experiencing failure. There can be no forgiveness or cleansing of unrighteousness if there is no confession (with the mouth) and repentance (the heartfelt act of making a 180-degree turn). This separates the individual from GOD. Unrepentant sin is also an unforgiven sin, leaving an individual in the clutches of darkness, which opposes GOD'S will. Many allow themselves to be unrepentant of their sins and deceive themselves into believing they have found lasting justification. They have become a law unto themselves. This is a difficult position to be in, especially for any believer. It is peculiar, but not in the manner that presents godly character and divine order. The enemy will use demonic influences to inhibit an individual's ability to discern what spirit is at work in them. So, the person is open to coming totally under the influence of a deceiving spirit. This is why the Lord is so set against pride. Pride was what Satan exhibited before being cast out of the presence of GOD.

GOD is light, and there is no darkness in Him. (1 John 1:5). Darkness is not only the opposite of light but also hates and avoids the light.

John 3:19-21 says,

And this is the condemnation that light is come into the world, and men loved darkness rather than light because their deeds were evil.

For everyone that doeth evil hateth the light, neither cometh to the light, lest his deeds should be reproved.

But he that doeth the truth cometh to the light, that his deeds may be made manifest, that they are wrought of GOD.

This war is being fought on the most unsuspected battlefield, which is the mind. It is a spiritual operation that transcends languages and culture. We no longer restrict ourselves to viewing battles and wars as traditional military conflicts. James 4:1-2 (NIV). This scripture tells us where wars originate. All wars and conflicts begin with,

1) Desires that battle within you.

2) Desires for what you cannot have, even being willing to kill for it.

3) You covet but cannot get what you want, so you quarrel and fight.

4) You do not have because you do not ask GOD.

Wars and conflicts have their grounding in darkness. Why? Because these wars are born out of evil motives. Since these works are evil, they remain hidden out of plain sight. As soon as these plans are discovered, they should be uprooted in a very timely fashion or before the most complex and destructive phases of their implementation begin. Then, the evil plot can be promptly averted.

This presents a problem with pinpointing the natural enemy. So, who is the enemy? Are you equipped and ready for this kind of battle? The answer should be yes! This war is a spiritual battle between light and darkness, good and evil. The light of truth, which is GOD'S glory, is being released to raise a standard against the enemy to decimate the darkness. Darkness hides, but light's assignment is to shine and illuminate every dark place to expose whatever is hidden. GOD is light, and His word is also light. (1 John 1:5; Psalm 119:105). Darkness cannot survive wherever light is present. The light of GOD is to never be turned off. When we walk into a dark house or room, the first thing that we usually do is to click on the nearest light switch so that we can see.

John 8:12 says,

Then spake Jesus again unto them, saying I am the light of the world. He that followeth Me shall not walk in darkness but shall have the light of life.

Matthew 5:14-16 KJV:

Ye are the light of the world. A city that is set on a hill cannot be hid.

Neither do men light a candle and put it under a bushel, but on a candlestick, and it giveth light unto all that are in the house.

Let your light so shine before men, that they may see your good works, and glorify your Father which is in heaven.

Darkness does not have the power to impose itself in such a way that it quenches or overtakes the light. The only way that darkness overshadows our light is when we retreat or withdraw from the place; we bring illumination.

The Apostle Paul prayed that our hearts would be flooded with light so that we would understand the confident hope He has given those He called holy people, who are His rich, glorious inheritance (Ephesians 1:18, New Living Translation NLT).

When our hearts are filled, flooded with the light of GOD'S word, which is His truth, then we are set to illuminate every place that we go with that same light. Light is not made to be hidden, but it reveals what lurks within the shadows of darkness. This is why GOD'S word was sent to heal, bring understanding, and destroy the works of darkness. The enemy does not want us to know and fully understand what we carry as the light of the world. Jesus refers to all true believers as the light of the world. (Matthew 5:14-16).

In Romans 13:12 ESV, the Apostle Paul says under the inspiration of the Holy Spirit,

The night is far gone; the day is at hand. So then let us cast off the works of darkness and put on the armor of light.

Remember, as a born-again believer, you are the light of the world!

Isaiah 60 speaks of the light of GOD'S glory that abides upon you. Glory no longer only abides upon us; it now abides within us. The Apostle Paul prayed that your heart be flooded with light. (Ephesians 1:18). The heart represents the inward part of man because our deeds proceed from the heart. So, whatever is in the heart will govern our direction in life. Will we be governed by the soul or the spirit? Our lives are to be dominated by the redemption of the soul and a renewed spirit given by GOD. The word of GOD is sharper than any double-edged sword. It penetrates even to divide or cut between soul and spirit. The light of GOD'S word shines, gives understanding, and makes a very clear distinction between what derives from the soul and what is from the spirit.

Arise, shine; For the light has come! And the glory of the Lord is risen upon you.

Where should the glory go? Answer: Where there is darkness.

For behold, the darkness shall cover the earth. And deep darkness the people. But the Lord will arise over you, and His glory will be seen upon you.

The Gentiles shall come to your light, and kings to the brightness of your rising.

Lift up your eyes all around, and see: They all gather together, they come to you; Your sons shall come from afar, and your daughters shall be nursed at your side.

Then you shall see and become radiant, and your heart shall swell with joy because the abundance of the sea shall be turned to you. The wealth of the Gentiles shall come to you.

We could have continued for the next few verses of this chapter, but the point was thoroughly made in verse 2; "But the Lord will arise over you." After that verse, darkness was not mentioned again in this chapter. Even though people existed in darkness, when the light of GOD'S glory was recognized, they began to be drawn to the light. The light of GOD is irresistible, whether it is embraced, or rejected. It is undefeatable or never overwhelmed unless it is withdrawn.

For we wrestle not against flesh and blood, but against principalities, and against powers, against the rulers of the darkness of this world, against spiritual wickedness in high places. (Ephesians 6:12 KJV).

We have been given weapons of warfare that are not carnal but are mighty to GOD to the pulling down of strongholds, casting down imaginations and every high thing that exalts itself against the knowledge of GOD. And bringing into captivity every thought unto the obedience of Jesus Christ. (2 Corinthians 10:4).

GOD Has a Plan for Your Life – For Such a Time As This

The world as we know it has already been positioned for a shift that the majority of the earth's population is unaware of. We are currently presented with enormous system failures which are causing a drastic exit from the old establishment. The word establishment in context, is composed of The Seven Mountains of Influence: 1) Business, 2) Arts and Entertainment, 3) Media, 4) Government, 5) Family, 6) Education, and 7) Religion. This great analogy was published by Creation House, in a remarkable book written by Johnny Enlow, called, The Seven Mountain Prophecy. Since these mountains exist, they must be overtaken and possessed for GOD'S Kingdom purposes.

Changing from something old and dysfunctional to something new is always a challenging transition to make. It will usually come with some turbulence and many uncomfortable situations. All arenas that we've found a sense of comfort and complacency in, will be shaken until they are done away with. Then, only the things which cannot be shaken will remain. (Hebrews 12:25-27 – NIV).

All changes will vary in their levels of complexity. They tend to challenge us and create an array of experiences that we've never seen before in our lifetime. Without them, we fail to grow in knowledge, as well as in acquiring wisdom and understanding along the way. The world is a combination of various cultural, religious, and socio-economic groups. Whether they differ in geographical locations, languages, or income statuses, they combine to make up a worldwide community. Please don't think that I'm making any reference to the community in the context of "one government for all." Governments as we've come to know, have seemingly sought to serve those living under their jurisdictions in the capacity of GOD. They develop our trust, through managing and dispensing vital resources that we all rely upon. Over the years, governments have taken on more of a bureaucratic approach in the way they serve. Most governments (local and abroad) have become extremely top-heavy and are usually ineffective in their service deliveries. No government on earth demonstrates true sensitivity and proper benevolence towards those they're authorized to serve. The design of government should be to exemplify or act as a representative of its people. A government in any form should always address the wills, needs, and desires of its people. Over time, we have witnessed a disintegration of governments' willingness to perform duties that provide services to every sovereign individual they represent. Even on the federal level, we witness a clear-cut dereliction to fulfill, even their constitutional duties. In GOD'S Kingdom, there is no such thing as an unfulfilled promise, or a promise unkept. 2 Corinthians1:20- 22 - NIV says,

For all the promises of GOD in Him are Amen to the glory of GOD through us.

Now He who establishes us with you in Christ and has anointed us in GOD.

Who also has sealed us and given us the Spirit in our hearts as a guarantee.

Hebrews 10:23 says,

Let us hold fast the profession of our faith without wavering (for He is faithful that promised.

The holy scriptures back up that GOD is bound by His Word because He cannot lie. (Titus 1:2). So, no matter what words GOD speaks out of His mouth, those words become living substances of the truth. The word of the Lord can never be denied. It is unconditional. In its proper context, that means that what GOD speaks and does is infallible, unchangeable, and immovable. One example of this is found in Genesis 8:21-22. It says,

And the Lord smelled a sweet savor, and the Lord said in His heart, I will not again curse the ground any more for man's sake, for the imagination of man's heart is evil from his youth; neither will I again smite any more everything living, as I have done.

While the earth remaineth, seedtime and harvest, and cold and heat, and summer and winter, and day and night shall not cease.

GOD also makes conditional promises as well. These conditional promises hinge upon Him giving an individual, group, or even a nation, a short window of time to correct any wrongs. Once that correction is made, it places them back into proper alignment.

Each day, the world moves closer to experiencing a series of cataclysmic events with major societal implications. Regardless of what category or group we identify with (nationality, tribe-racial, sexual orientation, rich, poor, etc.), we will all be greatly impacted. Although there are many divisions and differences in cultures and people groups, we are on a spiritual journey together, whether we fully acknowledge it or not.

Due to our interaction with the three-dimensional world, it can become difficult to discern beyond this realm.

This book is written to examine the concepts and principles that involve promotion on GOD'S terms. Certain principles work in the spirit realm that very easily translate into the physical or natural realm. Jesus Christ spoke of this in His dialogue with the disciples, quoted in the following verse in Matthew 6:10:

Thy kingdom come; thy will be done on earth as it is in heaven.

Finding My Identity on GOD'S Pathway

GOD'S plan is always uniquely different from the one that we would think of or choose for ourselves. As a child, I viewed myself as someone who didn't fit in well with the crowd. As a boy, I had a very narrow perspective of who I was. Through a culmination of experiences, I formed the attitude that everyone was bigger, smarter, self-confident, and more fluent in their expressions than I was. This was a time in my life when I didn't want to fit into that good kid mold that others seemed to place me in. I was genuinely who I was, but I learned what it took to be more acceptable to others, not just anyone. I was selective about whose behaviors I would emulate. Whenever I engaged in this form of acting, it only got me further away from my center, meaning who I genuinely was made to be. It was not working for me, which caused me to be like a fish attempting to live outside of its natural habitat.

I am so thankful that I came from a large family because that realization greatly assisted with keeping me somewhat grounded, and genuine. Having many sisters and brothers not only gave me this sense of who I was but also a greater appreciation of how unique and different GOD had made me. I can gladly say that I have never been estranged from my family in any way. I have an enduring love for each one of them.

The family is GOD'S idea. As a concept, family is one of the greatest privileges that GOD has given us to be a part of. It taught me to love and respect the rights, property, and privileges of others. It taught me about the importance of having order and not chaos. I learned that there were consequences for my behaviors, both good and bad. I learned how to communicate through negotiation, loving, and helping others. I also learned to complete assigned responsibilities along with many other things. I found that in a family, you learn to develop close alliances. Trusting bonds are formed with individuals with whom you share your most intimate secrets. You love them all, but the Lord knows who you may need for an exact time and occasion. Proverbs 17:17 NLT says that,

A friend is always loyal, and a brother is born to help in time of need.

We are commanded to love one another. We must not be the ones that instigate divisive actions towards people out of hurts, feelings, or disappointments that concern things they may have done to us. We must pray to our Father in Heaven for the strength and ability to forgive them, even as He has forgiven us. Maybe we don't think that we ever need to ask for forgiveness, because we're not aware of our wrongs. Believe me, we need forgiveness daily. If not, Jesus would not have included it in His model for praying to His Father in Heaven. Matthew 6:11-15 ESV says,

Give us this day, our daily bread.

And forgive us our debts as we also have forgiven our debtors.

And lead us not into temptation, but deliver us from evil.

For if you forgive others their trespasses, your heavenly Father will also forgive you.

But if you do not forgive others their trespasses, neither will your Father forgive your trespasses.

Regardless of the magnitude of the crime committed, any lingering unforgiveness will allow for a legal entry, making a pathway for demonic interferences in your life and relationships. The enemy will work through our emotional hurts and disappointments to hinder any spiritual growth and successful advancement in the Kingdom of GOD. We sometimes tend to think that the Kingdom of GOD means that you are in an official ministry. It seems foreign by church standards today. It is not a church thing at all, but it is a GOD thing. This is why we are to seek the Kingdom of GOD and His righteousness first, and then all the things we need will be added to us. GOD'S Kingdom should always come first!

Whenever I meditate on my given role in the expansion of GOD'S Kingdom, that alone helps me to know that there is a vastness to the will of the Lord's plan for my life and yours as well. It is not to stand out from others but to be an integral part of something far greater than you or I could ever do alone. Though it may require individual courage to step out and do it, someone is waiting in the wings for you to step into your position. As soon as you arrive at your designated post, ready to make your contribution, the body that you're a part of will function at maximum levels. You are such a vital part of that process.

While searching for my true identity, I was not ready to execute my function in the Kingdom of GOD. Why? Because I was imitating someone else. These were individuals that I looked up to. I allowed them to mentor and teach me to the extent of their limited knowledge. It would take years of much toil and frustration before I had a true encounter with my Lord and Savior, Jesus Christ. Being filled with the Holy Ghost forever changed my life for the better. My life was enhanced as I received this newly found love for GOD, myself, and others. It is a process, but GOD continues to engage me in removing self-inflicted limitations from my life. Imposed limitations of any kind serve as hindrances to positioning anyone for the Lord's promotion. Do you believe that you can be set free from imposed beliefs, attitudes, and impressions of others about you? If not, you need an encounter like Jeremiah had through the word of the Lord spoken to him. The words of the Lord countered and eventually changed Jeremiah's belief system.

What GOD said to Jeremiah (Jeremiah 1:4-5)

Then the word of the Lord came to me, saying:

Before I formed you in the womb, I knew you.

Before you were born, I sanctified you.

I ordained you a prophet to the nations.

What Jeremiah said to GOD (Jeremiah 1:6).

Then said I, Ah, Lord GOD! Behold, I cannot speak; for I am a child.

Jeremiah's words were not in agreement with GOD'S plan at first. Jeremiah spoke out of his mindset of limitations which he learned through culture and tradition. For the Lord will always operate outside of the boundaries of every limitation that worldly thinking seeks to impose. There was an old saying when adults were conversing together that children should be seen and not heard. Perhaps this traditional saying in that given culture had aided in formulating Jeremiah's perception of himself. Did this limited thinking prevent or hinder the call that was on young Jeremiah's life? No. There was much more that the Lord would say to him. Jeremiah 1:7-10 KJV:

But the Lord said unto me. Say not, I am a child: For thou shalt go to all that I shall send thee, and whatsoever I command thee thou shalt speak.

Be not afraid of their faces; for I am with thee to deliver thee, saith the Lord.

Then the Lord put forth His hand and touched my mouth. And the Lord said unto me. Behold, I have put My words in thy mouth.

See, I have this day set thee over the nations and over the kingdoms, to root out and to pull down and to destroy, and to throw down, to build, and to plant.

GOD had exclusively put His words in Jeremiah's mouth to boldly speak. He was commissioned not only to speak to a single people or nation but also to nations and to exert spiritual authority over kingdoms. Then the Lord articulated and clarified Jeremiah's role, and the purpose of his calling:

To root out and pull down and to destroy.

To throw down.

To build.

To plant.

What an awesome and powerful word from the Lord to a young man whom some historians have indicated to have been between the ages of 17 and 20. He could have easily forsaken his calling and gone after the lifestyle of his common peers. Still, the word of the Lord was activated in his heart, stirring the mighty calling and gifts that Jeremiah was anointed with.

Just as in any other institution, there are always orders Many requirements that lead to promotion in the Kingdom of GOD. Promotions take time to acquire. They usually come with tests and trials that will require your willingness, obedience, and patience. When there is a distinct calling in your life, the realization and implementation process may not always come at a time of convenience. It will usually disrupt what might be viewed as a comfortable lifestyle. I believe many called and anointed people may be in a hiding place of comfort. They may not fully realize they exist in this state of being, but they intuitively discern that GOD has more for them. I believe that GOD is bringing these people to the forefront. He will promote whomever He wills at the appointed time, just as He did with Esther.

Esther was a beautiful Hebrew girl raised as a daughter by her uncle, Mordecai. Both of her parents were deceased. So, as a father, Mordecai assumed full responsibility for Esther's welfare, ensuring she received the very best in life. They came into the Kingdom of Shushan at God's appointed time. This occurred Just as King Ahasuerus' kingdom was on the verge of a significant transition. It involved Queen Vashti's unwillingness to adhere to a simple request made by the king to appear before him, and others gathered for a time of merriment. Due to Queen Vashti's refusal to comply with the king's expectations, she decided to discharge the queen of her duties. So, efforts were made to seek out select virgins within the territory to replace the royal vacancy. At the appointed time, Esther, Mordecai, and the Hebrew people had recently come out of captivity and were migrating to Shushan to start anew. Mordecai ensured that Esther was included among the women preparing for the king's selection process to replace the vanquished queen. Esther quickly stood out among those selected and became the most favored by the king.

GOD anointed Esther to assume this position. The ultimate purpose of her positioning was to preserve life, in much the same manner as Joseph, when he was sold into slavery, imprisoned, and later exalted to the second most powerful position in all of that kingdom. There was time for preparation before each of their elevations. It was GOD'S doing in each scenario.

Even though Esther had become the Queen of Shushan, she did not realize the power and influence of her role and purpose for which she was strategically positioned. It was not until Mordecai posed the weighty circumstances of Israel's dilemma to her that she realized the seriousness of the matter. Without GOD positioning her to intervene on behalf of her people, all of Israel would have been destined to perish. The plan to destroy all of Esther's people was set in place by the conniving legal decree, which Haman had deviously created. King Ahasuerus had recently promoted Haman to a position above all the princes within his administration. Haman's heart was not right towards GOD nor towards His people. When Mordecai did not pay homage to Haman at the king's gate, a diabolical plot was hatched to kill not only him but all of his people. (Esther 3:2-6). Unbeknownst to the king, he was deceived into placing his seal on the decree crafted by Haman, making it an irrevocable law to destroy all of the children of Israel, which also would include his queen and wife, Esther. Mordecai began by informing Esther of Haman's evil plan to destroy GOD'S people. Initially, Esther was unwilling to step outside the kingdom's protocols to aid in averting this inevitable disaster for her people. Mordecai further appealed to Esther in the following scriptures:

Then Mordecai commanded to answer Esther. Think not with thyself that thou shalt escape in the king's house more than all the Jews.

For if thou altogether holdest thy peace at this time, then shall there enlargement and deliverance arise to the Jews from another place; but thou and thy father's house shall be destroyed, and who knoweth whether thou art come to the kingdom for such a time as this? (Esther 4:13-15 KJV).

For the first time, Esther realized that she was strategically placed to preserve not only the lives of her people but generations for their posterity's sake. I love how Esther responds to this. She commanded Mordecai to gather all of the Jews in Shushan for a three-day fast for her preparation to go before the king. This would be attempted outside of the normal protocols or laws of the kingdom. So, on the third day, Esther put on her royal apparel and stood in the inner court of the king's house as he sat on his royal throne in the royal house over against the gate of the house. When the king saw her stunning elegance and beauty, Esther obtained favor in his sight. The king then held out the golden scepter that was in his hand. So, Esther then drew near and touched the top of the scepter.

Thank GOD for the wisdom that Esther exhibited. She was highly knowledgeable and respectful of all the protocols and procedures that pertained to the laws of that kingdom. Though her efforts to save her people did not follow the requirements to approach the king, Esther showed great courage. She was adequately prepared to risk even her life if King Ahasuerus refused to grant her favor to gain his presence.

We approach the King of Kings and Lord of Lords in the same manner as Esther. We approach Him with a prepared heart and with the highest of regards. The plan of the heart belongs to man, but the answer of the tongue is from the Lord. (Proverbs 16:1 ESV). Although Esther's actions were taken out of her desperation to make a life-sacrificing plea on behalf of her people, Israel, GOD had already gone before her to prepare her for this divine moment in time. She followed suit with the plan, but GOD had already provided the answer. He was only waiting for Esther to step into that moment. She not only showed great courage but absolute humility towards GOD first. Esther requested that corporate prayer and fasting be made to GOD by her and her maidens and all of Israel for three days before she approached the king.

We, too, are given open access to freely approach the throne of our Father in heaven with confidence and boldness. What makes this possible? Is it based on our efforts, or is it by grace which was acquired and granted on behalf of those who willingly receive it? Hebrews 4:14-16 (KJV) gives us the answer.

Seeing then that we have a great high priest that is passed into the heavens, Jesus the Son of GOD, let us hold fast our profession.

For we have not an high priest which cannot be touched with the feeling of our infirmities; but was in all points tempted like as we are, yet without sin.

Let us therefore come boldly unto the throne of grace, that we may obtain mercy, and find grace to help in time of need.

So, as our High Priest, Jesus Christ Himself has given us the access that we must have to approach the heavenly throne of GOD Almighty to make our petitions known. We also come before Him to offer up our most intimate sacrifices of praise and worship with a heart of thanksgiving. One of the significant keys to preparing for promotion is to walk in humility, knowing that without the mercies and grace of GOD, we cannot acquire the things that make lasting impact in the lives of others, even having impacts that influence generations. When we follow GOD'S ways of doing things, we have the blueprint and the assurance that our posterity will remain intact for generations to come. When we see the significance of following His precepts, we can be confident that we have indeed left an inheritance to our children and their children's children, and so on.

Prideful Motives will be Removed

The devil will always use various avenues to gain a legal entrance into any situation or individual's life. How does this happen? There are spiritual laws that are always at work, those that give access to GOD'S will, and those that leave an open door for evil works to emerge—in the case of Haman, pride and a haughty spirit contributed to his ultimate ruin. These attributes come from the father of lies. When Lucifer allowed these attributes to overtake him in the heavenly realms, it warranted his expulsion (along with a third of the angels) from the presence of GOD. We must always be careful of who or what is near us. Be spiritually sensitive. Ask the Lord to sharpen your discernment of spirits and know how to defend against the enemy's subtle persuasions prayerfully.

Proverbs 16:18-19 says,

Pride goes before destruction and a haughty spirit before a fall.

Better to be of a humble spirit with the lowly, than to divide the spoil with the proud.

In the Book of Esther, Haman exemplifies how some people mishandle promotion due to their pride. Haman allowed his promotion by King Ahasuerus, which set him above all the princes in the kingdom, to give him a false opinion of his importance. This was merely based on his ascension over all the princes in the kingdom. Rather than rightfully embracing the position of authority, he used it to satisfy his inordinate need for power and illicit control. Thus, this led to the exposure of his flawed character and corrupt heart. Pride allowed the enemy to gain access to Haman's life. Remember, the devil's whole purpose is to steal, kill, and destroy. He has only been a liar and a murderer from the beginning.

This is a critical hour for those within the church world. Some of today's organized churches or denominations have readily practiced methods of promoting individuals through institutional politics, self-promotion, favoritism, financial influence, family affiliations, etc. There must be caution applied when any appointment involves the exercise of managing or forms of governing others. Authority comes from GOD, but man sabotaged what the Lord ordained by corrupting what had divine intent. I am not in any way saying that promotions under the auspices of organized or institutional settings are unwarranted. Promotions should be based on just and righteous standards when they are warranted.

The word "churchdom" comes to mind when I think of how the established framework of the institutional church has sought to supplant the true church, which Jesus Christ refers to in Matthew 16:13-18 KJV:

When Jesus came unto the coasts of Caesarea Philippi, He asked His disciples, saying, whom do men say that I the Son of man am?

And they said some say that Thou art John the Baptist. Some say Elijah, and others, Jeremiah or one of the prophets.

He saith unto them; but whom say ye that I am?

And Simon Peter answered and said, Thou art the Christ, the Son of the Living GOD.

And Jesus answered and said unto him, Blessed art thou, Simon Barjona. For flesh and blood hath not revealed it unto thee, but My Father which is in heaven.

And I say also unto thee, that thou art Peter, and upon this rock I will build My church; and the gates of hell shall not prevail against it.

Some religious circles believe that Jesus was referring to Peter since the Hebrew name for Peter is Petra, which means "rock." Jesus was not referring to Peter but to Peter's revelation of who He was: Jesus Christ, the Son of the Living GOD.

Would it be consistent with spiritual law for GOD to give that much credence to a mortal man to serve as the foundation for the Body of Christ/His Son? It was the revelation of Jesus being the Christ, the Son of the living GOD, that the church would be built upon. The word of GOD is a firm, everlasting foundation that prevails against the powers of darkness. For the gates of hell will never prevail against it. Jesus Christ took on the sins of the whole world, redeeming us from the curse of the law, becoming a curse for us. Everyone was considered cursed and was hanged on a tree. (Galatians 3:13). We must daily acknowledge that Jesus took what rightfully should have been our place. He became sin, who knew no sin so that we might be made the righteousness of GOD through Him. (2 Corinthians 5:21). We must see a place of humility with thanksgiving for what Jesus Christ has done for us. By grace, we are made accessible, not by our abilities or good works. We must know with great certainty that it is the gift of GOD. By knowing this, it eliminates all pride and self-righteousness from our midst.

Churchdom or Kingdom – Is There a Competition?

Churchdom is only some of what it may sound like. It refers to the church as an entity that establishes, implements, and governs itself within religious principles. Churchdom functions within the boundaries of time, schedules, and programs. It allows for sprinkling rather than for the rains of the Holy Spirit. I equate it with the symbolism of a herd of beautiful, untamed white horses running freely in the winds of the vast western plains. Horse ranchers who gain legal access to the herds seek to harvest these beautiful creatures from their natural habitation to harness their power for personal use. They successfully capture the herd, transferring them to their ranch. They corral, break, or tame them there, causing them to conform to their owner's specific needs. The Holy Spirit can never be corralled or harnessed because He is uncontainable. He wasn't merely sent by Jesus, as in John 14:15-31. The bottom line is that the Holy Spirit is GOD. Yes, GOD is in the earth, living inside every believer who receives Him. Jesus Christ sent the Holy Spirit to lead and guide us into all truth. He desires that His will be done in all of the earth. If we are willing to participate in that plan, we must yield to the Holy Spirit. An assembly of people gathered together under the influence of the Holy Spirit is the counter to Churchdom's survival. It is a requirement of the Kingdom of GOD. Those whom the Spirit of GOD leads are sons of GOD. In many cases, churchdom strongly resembles what would appear very pleasing to GOD, but instead, it boils down to being merely a formality. How does this take place? Satan sends his secret agents to infiltrate the houses of the Lord to dilute the power and presence of the Holy Spirit. This did not occur suddenly but was done little by little, subtly, and without notice, one house at a time. We have experienced a hijacking of what was once faithful to the faith and simplicity of the gospel of the Kingdom of Christ. Churchdom is in no way comparable to the Kingdom of GOD because its main focus is to preserve an institutional structure that conveniently claims Jesus' headship. Although it emulates many of the traditional tenets, it threatens to make Christianity more of a religion than a spirit-led lifestyle. A great compromise is in progress within the walls of so-called Churchdom. The standards for truth and morality once held so highly, have become past tense and irrelevant in the current scheme of operations. The Holy Spirit has long vacated this hijacked, worldly, infiltrated version of the church. Ephesians 4:30-32 NIV says,

And do not grieve the Holy Spirit of GOD, by whom you were sealed for the day of redemption.

Get rid of all bitterness, rage, anger, brawling, and slander, along with every form of malice.

Be kind and compassionate to one another, forgiving each other, just as in Christ GOD forgave you.

The Holy Spirit will not stay in an environment where He cannot function. Whenever the flesh is more prevalent, the Holy Spirit will never compete with that. He always yields to our will. When we are willing to surrender to His presence, the Holy Spirit is free to demonstrate the power of GOD.

Any disruption of the current structural definition of the church would be considered highly controversial and, more than likely, unacceptable when referring to the Kingdom of God. In any case, we must not allow the church to become a cheap imitation of God's house, denying the Holy Spirit's true power. This is territorial trespass for many established churches because many have frequently been possessive of people and not as supportive and engaged in their overall development outside of the four walls.

GOD'S Business of Promoting and Demoting

In the book of Esther, several examples are given to us of how GOD sets one up and sets down another. Rather than starting with Esther, I will briefly focus on Haman's rise to power. It came on the heels of the investigation and prosecution of the two men who planned the murder of the king. Of course, without the efforts of Mordecai to quickly report his findings, the entire kingdom could have possibly fallen into devastation. Rather than Mordecai receiving proper recognition, Haman became the beneficiary. Mordecai reported his findings to Queen Esther, and she informed King Ahasuerus in Mordecai's name; it was somehow overlooked. So, it would be fair to say that Haman's timely promotion was due to Mordecai. (Esther 3:23). It is always consistent with the devil's plan to usurp position and authority. GOD had a plan in all of this. What appeared to look like the unrighteous were getting the upper hand; GOD'S plan would prevail. Mordecai would eventually receive recognition and a proper reward right in the presence of his enemy.

The true motivations of Haman's heart became manifest in the moment that his authority was challenged. This dark and devious spirit did not emerge until Mordecai refused to give Haman the proper recognition at the king's gate. Just as the three Hebrew boys refused to honor the king's decree to bow to the king's golden image (Daniel 3:14-25), Mordecai refused to bow to Haman.

This was a matter that Haman allowed to fester. So, he used it as an opportunity to set a plan to destroy Mordecai. He initiated this plan by first going to the king to inform him of a man within the kingdom who defied their laws. King Ahasuerus gave Haman his signet ring as his authorized stamp or seal for this official decree. Once he found that the Jews were his people, the devil sought to exterminate all of them in one day. Please see the following scriptures:

Esther 3:13-15 KJV says,

And the letters were by posts into all the king's provinces, to destroy, to kill and to cause to perish all Jews, both young and old, little children and women, in one day, even upon the thirteenth day of the twelfth month, which is the month of Adar. And to take the spoil of them for prey.

The copy of the writing for a commandment to be given in every province was published unto all people, that they should be ready against that day.

The posts went out, hastened by the king's command, and the decree was given in Shushan's palace. The king and Haman sat down to drink, but the city of Shushan was perplexed.

Haman's behavior exhibited his heart was filled with prideful motives. His position was used as a tool for the devil to gain a more accessible avenue to destroy GOD'S people. Due to Haman's pride and misuse of authority, GOD brought him down. As the scripture states, "GOD sets one up, and He sets down another." (Psalm 75:7). Mordecai exhibited loyalty, courage, and humility, which the king noted on one of his sleepless nights. When King Ahasuerus reviewed his chronicles that night, it came to his attention that Mordecai had discovered a plot to assassinate him. When Mordecai made this information known to the royal authorities, they were successful in averting the assassination plot and, as a result, saved the life of the king. Mordecai received recognition for his loyalty to the throne. The king chose to honor the man whom Haman most despised. GOD caused this remarkable recognition to be displayed in the presence of Mordecai's and Israel's major enemies. (Esther 6:6-14).

Mordecai's Reward

Once Esther revealed Haman's diabolical plan to exterminate all of the Jews, including herself, King Ahasuerus turned the tables on him. What ended up being meant for Mordecai and the Jews ended up being the fate of Haman. He was hung on the same gallows that he had ordered to be built. Further, Esther once again found favor in the eyes of the king when she requested a letter be written to revoke all Haman's letters, rendering the total annihilation of the Jews. King Ahasuerus granted her request, giving her the house of Haman. Esther set Mordecai over Haman's house.

So, Mordecai went out from the presence of the king in royal blue and white apparel with a great crown of gold and a garment of fine linen and purple, and the city of Shushan rejoiced and was glad. (Esther 8:15 NIV).

Mordecai was elevated to the place that Haman had once occupied. GOD saw what he did when no one else was watching and rewarded him for his loyalty and godly integrity.

Earlier, I referred to the modern-day church using "churchdom." This reference was made because the church was not considered an institution but a functioning body that belonged solely to Jesus Christ. Jesus said in Matthew 6:33 ESV,

But seek first the kingdom of GOD and His righteousness, and all these things will be added to you.

The main point being made is to put the Kingdom of GOD first. People ask, "What is the Kingdom of GOD?" Romans 14:17 says,

For the Kingdom of GOD is not meat and drink, but righteousness, peace, and joy in the Holy Ghost.

"Churchdom" is not likened to the Kingdom of GOD. It is my personal word choice used to describe an artificial infiltration of the church. Churchdom is the flesh's attempt to imitate the actual Body of Christ. Since no flesh and blood can inherit GOD'S Kingdom, any effort that is made to overthrow what is Holy Spirit initiated would self-destruct. The enemy uses systems of failed attempts to weaken and capture the church, making the church void of any real significance and true power. Those who are spiritually alert have an inner witness that the church is being held captive by a religious order rather than the Holy Spirit. We must have the Holy Spirit to empower the church to do the more wondrous works that our Lord and Savior refers to in John 14:12. Without Him, our efforts may be noble but are not enough to produce the fruit of the Spirit in its members. The Holy Spirit-led church is powerful. For it fully identifies with GOD in Christ Jesus and defies the works of the flesh, a poor imitation of the Spirit of GOD. Religion cannot survive on its own. It is the equivalent of idolatry and divination due to its extreme aversion to what is unable to be contained. The church as we know it in our society has been held captive within walls of tradition and indoctrination. What is the evidence that the church has been captured? We have seen a carnal church that has conformed to the influences of the world system. The health crisis revealed this for many of our congregations in the USA and worldwide. The church capitulated to the fear-mongering and false information and hid the light of the truth rather than sharing that light as the world became darker and darker. Therefore, we witnessed more of what a powerless, faithless, and loveless demonstration of the alternative to the house of GOD should be. During the time of the pandemic (2019-2023), most churches reacted to government-induced fear tactics, being traumatized and taken captive along with the majority of other primary institutions. The church was minimized to being a mere shadow of its once influential status in shaping society. What was once great was dwindling to become a cheap imitation of the true church Jesus Christ referred to in Matthew 16:13-18. What I am saying may be controversial, but it is based on what is seen as the church in decline. The spirit of religion has infiltrated and detrimentally weakened the true church, creating its image of what the worship of GOD should be. This does not mean all churches intentionally antagonize Jesus' teachings. On the day of Jesus Christ, religious factions worshipped the same GOD in two separate ways. One with the power of the Holy Spirit and the other without the Holy Spirit's intervention.

Jesus came to the earth so that we might have life and have it more abundantly. He also said that He must return to His Father so that the Holy Spirit could be sent to empower the Body of Christ. Jesus did not come to destroy what was referred to as the Law of Moses but to fulfill them. Jesus Christ redeemed man from the curse of the law, being made a curse. He assumed all of the world's sins for those who would receive the grace of God's forgiveness. Salvation would no longer be temporal but eternal through the blood of Jesus Christ. Jesus came to make a clear difference between the laws that Moses received from GOD and the law of the Spirit of life, which makes men free from the law of sin and death.

Hebrews 8:6-13 NIV says,

But now He has obtained a more excellent ministry since He is also a Mediator of a better covenant, which was established on better promises.

For if that first covenant had been faultless then no place would have been sought for a second.

Because finding fault with them, He says, "Behold, the days are coming says the Lord when I will make a new covenant with the house of Israel and with the house of Judah.

Not according to the covenant, I made with their fathers in the day when I took them by the hand and led them out of the land of Egypt, because they did not continue in My covenant, and I disregarded them, says the Lord.

I will put My laws in their minds and write them on their hearts, and I will be their GOD, and they shall be My people.

None of them shall teach his neighbor and none his brother, saying, "Know the Lord;"

For all shall know Me from the least of them to the greatest of them.

For I will be merciful to their unrighteousness, and their sins and their lawless deeds I will remember no more.

In that He says, "A new covenant," He has made the first obsolete. Now what is becoming obsolete and growing old is ready to vanish away.

Is It a Waiting Game, or Is It For Your Development?

When we acquire patience, it makes us complete and entire, lacking nothing. (James 1:4). Patience is developed when we are willing to wait to obtain something of great value. What we highly anticipate could either be tangible or intangible. It is better whenever it is attached to one of GOD'S promises. Evidence is always found in what you're hoping for. Without having an expectation, then there is no true destination. We will not wonder aimlessly if there are high expectations. If there is no expectation, then all hope is deferred. There must be something of substance to hope for patience to be employed. Faith is the substance of things hoped for, the evidence of things not seen. (Hebrews 11:1). Without patience, we cannot obtain the promises we hope for. We are not to be slothful in our efforts to follow the examples of those in the scriptures, who served as examples of how to obtain GOD'S promises through faith and patience. I have seen many people preach from the pulpit or in conversation and say that if what you believe GOD to do in your life situation does not happen over time, you must not be in the faith. In essence, it could easily be that in this particular situation, you haven't exercised or acquired the patience to receive what GOD promised.

Hebrews 6:11-13 - KJV says,

And we desire that every one of you do shew the same diligence to the full assurance of hope unto the end.

That ye be not slothful, but followers of them who through faith and patience inherit the promises.

For when GOD made promise to Abraham because he could swear by no greater, He sware by Himself.

GOD cannot help but to deliver on every one of His promises. He is incapable of reneging on any of the promises that He speaks. Why? He is the most sovereign, supreme authority, ruler, and power. This remains true, even today and for all of eternity.

GOD never just randomly gives out promotions based on our potential alone. He knows exactly what has been placed within you; that includes your gifts and all. Nothing in you and me is just randomly given. They are directly connected to our purpose for being here. We sometimes go through life without realizing we are given specific gifts to complement our calling. The question is, are gifts and particular callings enough to prove our worthiness and sustain us in our spiritual walk? The answer cannot always be answered in the affirmative. Neither do gifts and callings alone have the depth or capacity to establish us in our long-term spiritual maturation. Spiritual maturity and godly character are most valued in the Kingdom of GOD. The scripture found in Psalm 75:6-7 says,

For promotion cometh neither from the east nor from the west, nor from the south.

But GOD is the judge: He putteth down one and setteth up another.

What stands out to me is what I see in verse 7, which says, *"But GOD is the judge: He putteth down one and setteth up another."*

This shows that GOD is highly serious and particular about who and when He promotes or demotes.

Let's take a look back at the time when Israel wanted their first king. (1 Samuel 8:5). At that time, the prophet Samuel was serving GOD as judge and priest over Israel. He had grown old, so he set his two sons, Joel and Abiah as priests over Israel. They proved untrustworthy and corrupt as representatives of the Most High GOD. This was very synonymous with the two sons of Eli when they, too, inherited their posts as priests over the people of Israel. Hophni and Phineas were corrupt men who openly displayed their high dishonor for the Lord's house and His people. Eli was reprimanded, not only for his son's outlandish behaviors but for giving more honor to his sons than he did to GOD. That was the word of the Lord to him through the man of GOD. So, the Lord had to send His word to shine the light of truth on what was being done under the veil of religion. This is what we see so much of today. What starts so innocently and with small beginnings grows and suddenly finds its way into the mainstream of modern church culture. At the same time that religion creates its atmosphere of spirituality, it makes unmistakable efforts to quench the Spirit of GOD. It seeks to emulate what is real by creating an artificial sensory experience designed to appeal to your emotions. There is an environment that religion must make to thrive. That is an atmosphere that emulates the Spirit but, in reality, is filled with barriers and controls. In this man-created culture, there is no evidence of the Holy Spirit's presence.

GOD sent His word unto Eli through a prophet to pronounce an end to what was ruled by their carnal appetites rather than from a hunger for the Lord. Here, GOD'S living word shed light on the deeds of these corrupt spiritual leaders, who committed sexual sins with the women and misused the offerings for their gain. In 1 Samuel 2:34-36 KJV, the word of the Lord said,

And this shall be a sign unto thee, that shall come upon thy sons, on Hophni and Phinehas, in one day they shall die, both of them.

And I will raise Me up a faithful priest, that shall do according to that which is in Mine heart and in My mind: and I will build him a sure house, and he shall walk before Mine anointed forever.

And it shall come to pass, that every one that is left in thine house shall come and crouch to him for a piece of silver and a morsel of bread, and shall say Put me, I pray thee, into one of the priests' offices, that I may eat a piece of bread.

The people soon complained to Samuel about his son's ungodly behaviors and asked him to give them a king like the surrounding nations. Of course, this grieved Samuel's heart, but God urged him to give the people what they requested. Before the transition, the Lord wanted Israel to know precisely what their king would require of them. Although the king's terms and methods of exerting his authority and leadership would prove very intrusive, Israel remained determined.

A Benjamite named Saul and one of his father's servants were sent to find lost donkeys. Due to the difficulty experienced in finding their missing animals, the men sought out the seer, or the prophet, Samuel. GOD spoke in the ear of the prophet, saying,

Tomorrow about this time, I will send to you a man from the land of Benjamin, and you shall anoint him to be prince over my people Israel. He shall save My people from the hand of the Philistines. For I have seen My people because their cry has come to Me. (1 Samuel 9:16 - ESV).

We now continue to 1 Samuel 10:1, which says,

Then Samuel took a flask of oil and poured it on his head and kissed him and said, "Has not the Lord anointed you to be prince over His people Israel? And you shall reign over the people of the Lord, and you will save them from the hand of their surrounding enemies. And this shall be the sign to you that the Lord has anointed you to be prince over his heritage. The anointing was given to equip Saul for his appointed service which was to be rendered unto the people of GOD. The King of Israel was ordained to defend this nation of choice. He was given the anointing to enhance GOD'S abilities to serve, protect, and provide for those under his authority. The anointing gave him the ability to defend Israel from its enemies. GOD knew that as His people dwelled in a continual environment of safety, they would prosper and flourish. Samuel was tasked with being a prophetic voice and a spiritual counsel to King Saul. Saul's anointing was not to be a priest, but a prince/king. If he ever stepped outside of what GOD had anointed him for, it could prove disastrous for the entire nation. This error would lead to an unproductive end to his rule of this great nation that GOD raised. So, the anointing did not build character or increase Saul's depth of wisdom or reverence for the Lord.

Over time, Saul acted independently of the instructions that came from the Lord. Due to his violation of the boundaries of his function, Saul lost the original intensity that the anointing provided to continue as King. He misappropriated the anointing. The season was too critical for GOD'S people to be left as vulnerable prey for their enemies. The Lord did not desire a leader who was driven to rule by the arm of the flesh, as Saul proved he would do. An unction or anointing from the Holy One is made available to every believer called and chosen by our Lord and Savior, Jesus Christ. The anointing gives us a comprehension of who GOD is and how to reach a greater agreement with His plans for kingdom purposes. This should not be for any selfish gain of our own. As said before, being anointed for service does not increase your capacity for love, faith, patience, reverence, or ability to obey the Lord. If we truly love GOD, we develop consistency in doing what He says to us. (John 14:15-31; 1 John 5:1-5).

David recognized how to respect both Saul's crown as king and the anointing that was given to him for service. He faithfully served a king who treated him so unjustly without cause. David went from being highly honored to being ill-treated. This change in how Saul approached David began during a festive celebration of another victory over their enemies. Saul's jealousy of young David was noted from the day that he saw and heard the women sing and play, "Saul has slain his thousands, and David his ten thousand." Saul became infuriated, saying,

"They have ascribed to David ten thousand, and to me, they have ascribed thousands, what more can he have but the kingdom?" And Saul eyed David from that day on. (1 Samuel 18:8-9 ESV).

David never dishonored Saul or showed the least hint of disloyalty to him. He wouldn't take Saul's armor when it was given to him to fight against the giant, Goliath. He never sought to stand in a position that was not his to possess until the appointed, perfect timing of GOD. David refused to touch who was once GOD'S anointed king. He did so up until the last breath that Saul took. We should never seek, or covet what belongs to someone else. The Lord so strongly despises this ungodly attribute that He included it among the Ten Commandments given to Moses. There is so much envy, jealousy, and covetousness being exercised within the ranks of the modern-day church, that it is difficult to recognize it as the house of prayer.

Knowing the Holy One is synonymous with having the mind of Jesus Christ. Everyone has their level of maturity in which they function. Your maturity level can never be faked. Situations will always arise to expose or locate our positioning and level of maturity, which the Holy Spirit grants. He is the one who teaches and leads us into all truth. My level of spiritual maturity should determine how I respond to anyone, whether they display godly or ungodly character.

In Leadership and Life - Love is Obedience to GOD

GOD is love. So, everything that He does flows through that unfailing law that is above every other law that operates in this earthly realm. He loved the world so much that He sent His only begotten Son. So that whosoever believes in Him should not perish but will have everlasting life. (John 3:16). We are not privileged to know all of the interactions Jesus had with His disciples, but we have a good idea of what He emphasized the most: His Father's love. Jesus taught this through His example of loving others as GOD loves. John 14:7-9 gives us a view of how focused Jesus was in demonstrating the will of His Father in Heaven.

If ye had known Me, ye should have known My father also: and from henceforth ye know him, and have seen Him.

Phillip saith unto him, Lord, show us the Father, and it sufficeth us.

Jesus saith unto him, Have I been so long time with you, and yet hast thou not known Me, Phillip? He that hath seen Me hath seen the Father; and how sayest thou then, show us the Father?

Walking in the love of GOD begins with deciding to follow the Lord's example. GOD'S love can only proceed from the heart or the level that the Holy Spirit can abide in a person's life. Romans 5:5 NIV says,

Now hope does not disappoint, because the love of GOD has been poured out in our hearts by the Holy Spirit who was given to us.

Jesus gave us two commandments on which all of the laws given by His Father in Heaven hang. They are the foundation and base upon which all laws are built. Without them, none of the other laws can stand. Matthew 22:37-40 KJV says,

Jesus said unto him (a lawyer),

Thou shalt love the Lord thy GOD with all thy heart, and with all thy soul, and with all thy mind.

This is the first and greatest commandment.

And the second is like unto it. Thou shalt love thy neighbor as thyself.

On these two commandments hang all the law and the prophets.

Love Always Does These Things

Suffers long (Patient),

Is kind.

Does not envy.

Does not boast.

Is not proud.

Does not parade itself.

Is not puffed up.

Do not behave rudely.

Does not seek its own.

Thinks no evil.

Does not rejoice in iniquity.

Rejoices in the truth.

Bears all things.

80

Dennis J. Perkins

Believes all things.

Hopes all things.

Endures all things.

Love never fails.

Spiritual maturity is one of the most important prerequisites that an individual should possess. Remember, this is a spiritual journey. GOD has precise directives. He never forces anyone to take heed or follow Him. We have to be willing to seek Him with our whole hearts. As our Heavenly Father, GOD will not take us to appointed destinations without our agreeing with His purpose for our life. We must have a willingness to be duly prepared for the journey. It would seem very inappropriate for GOD to force His purposes on us. Can you visualize a kindergarten teacher forcibly dragging a child from their classroom to the sixth-grade classroom as they kick and scream in resistance? Is that child ready to be promoted? I don't think so. By usual academic standards, kindergarteners would not be considered promotable until they meet all requirements and are academically proficient in all areas. As stated earlier, potential alone doesn't qualify anyone for promotion. Some school students advance several grades when they perform at higher academic levels. Although students' test results were high, some were not emotionally mature enough to remain on that grade level.

You cannot expect to possess and maintain things in the Kingdom of GOD with an inadequacy-based mindset. The only way to have the life of the Kingdom of GOD is to ascend to higher levels and encounters in the spirit, in your thinking, faith, knowledge base, and lifestyle. Romans 12:2 New International Version (NIV).

Do not conform to the pattern of this world, but be transformed by the renewing of your mind. Then, you will be able to approve what GOD'S will is.-His good, pleasing, and perfect will.

Qualities That Lead the Way to Promotion

Some primary character traits lay a strong foundation that can lead to promotion. They are simple building blocks that parents should instill in their children, provided the parents do their part, and the children take heed of their instructions.

- Wisdom – Proverbs 4:5-8 says,

  Get wisdom, get understanding; forget it not; neither decline from the words of my mouth.

  Forsake her not, and she shall preserve thee; love her, and she shall keep thee.

  Wisdom is the principal thing. Therefore, get wisdom, and in all thy getting, get understanding.

  Exalt her, and she shall promote thee. She shall bring thee to honor when thou dost embrace her.

  As a young man, Solomon was crowned King of Israel. He was not presumptuous but knew the magnitude of his responsibility as king. So, when GOD appeared to him and asked what he desired, King Solomon did not ask for a long life, for greater wealth, or even for the destruction of his enemies. Instead, he asked GOD to give him an understanding heart to rightfully judge His people and that he could discern between good and evil.

- Knowledge – Proverbs 1:7 says,

The fear of the Lord is the beginning of knowledge, but fools despise wisdom and instruction.

Psalm 119:66 is a prayer request of the psalmist. He says,

Teach me good judgment and knowledge: For I have believed your commandments.

- Faith – Abraham was referred to as the father of faith. He was presented with the word of the Lord. He put all of his trust in GOD'S word to him. Romans 4:20-25 says,

He staggered not at the promise of GOD through unbelief but was strong in faith, giving glory to GOD.

And being fully persuaded that, what He had promised, He was able to also perform.

And therefore, it was imputed to him for righteousness.

Now it was not written for his sake alone, that it was imputed to him.

But for us also to whom it shall be imputed if we believe on Him that raised up Jesus our Lord from the dead:

Who was delivered for our offenses and was raised for our justification.

- Integrity—Integrity is one of the most important godly characteristics an individual could ever possess. Proverbs 11:3 (NIV) says, "The *integrity of the upright guides them, but their duplicity destroys the unfaithful.*"

A person who walks with true integrity should not be found to be deceitful or double-dealing. Integrity is one of the most desirable ingredients for sound relationships, whether family-related or work-related. Those walking in integrity are always dependable. They accept responsibility wholeheartedly and try to improve or upgrade their immediate environment.

- Humility – Some people aspire to have positions of importance but do not acquire the patience or skill set to get them to the destiny that they dream of. Proverbs 18:12 says,

Before destruction, the heart of a man is haughty. And before honor is humility.

Living a life governed by self-centeredness, self-exaltation, and pride is destructive. GOD will always resist pride. There are no shortcuts or avoidances, but He gives His grace to the humble in spirit. Many people in this society have a distorted view of success. Some even use tactics of manipulation, which is a form of spiritual witchcraft, to expedite their rise to a position of prominence. They violate the sanctity and value of what could prove to be a true godly relationship.

- Love – Love will always cover a multitude of sins. So, we know that there is not a condemning aspect of love. Love is associated with the purity and intimacy of GOD'S heart towards all that He has created. Man was made and fashioned in the image of GOD. The Lord took precious time walking with Adam in the cool of the day to be that example of what love is. Love is never forced but is freely given and freely received. There are no stipulations other than to keep GOD'S commandments. Jesus said, If you love Me, keep My commandments, or do what I say. As parents model behavior for their children to follow, so does the Lord when we take walks with Him in the cool of the day. We, like no other creation of GOD, were given sonship status. That is in no way disparaging to you sisters out there. Regarding having sonship with GOD, it has no reference to gender but is plural. It is being referred to in a plural sense.

Genesis 1:27 says,

So, GOD created man in His own image, in the image of GOD created He him; male and female created He them.

And GOD blessed them, and GOD said unto them,

Be fruitful and multiply and replenish the earth and subdue it, and have dominion over the fish of the sea, and over the fowl of the air and over every living thing that moveth upon the earth.

We know that GOD is Spirit, and they that worship Him MUST worship Him in spirit and truth. (John 4:24). He is not a man that He should lie, neither is He the son of man that He should repent; Has He said, and shall He not do it? Or has He spoken, and shall He not make it good? (Numbers 23:19). Is there any other reason that man is the only creature in GOD'S creation that has been given commandments to love? Why? It is not a complex question. Since GOD has given us the capacity to love, GOD confidently gives us commandments to love Him and others as we love ourselves. Many people find it very difficult to love themselves. Jesus commanded us to love our neighbor as ourselves, the second commandment He gave to His followers, the apostles. (Matthew 22:36-40). So, as the apostles first received love, they learned to abide in that love, and freely communicate the degree of love which abided within them. Their ability to love was greatly enhanced when they were filled with the Holy Spirit on the Day of Pentecost. The love of GOD entered into their hearts by the power of the Holy Ghost. (Romans 5:5). Communication is an open dialogue between two or more people. GOD does not view us as a group of people; He intimately knows each of us.

All transformations require a change of environmental surroundings. How can true change manifest in an individual's life if they frequent old places to indulge in all their familiar activities? We must break away from old, familiar patterns to fully commit to change.

Where are We Going? How Do We Get There? Are We There Yet?

The question often comes to mind; "Where is the Kingdom of GOD?" Is it in a specific geographical location? Is it somewhere above the Earth's atmosphere? Unless you're a new student of the Holy Bible, you should already know that the answer to these questions is, no, it is not. It isn't very easy to follow instructions on how to get to a place without having the directions that lead you to that location. We are not in the process of following a yellow brick road to seek and find this kingdom. It is not a place that is built with hands. It never ages or deteriorates because it is eternally housed within all those who believe that GOD raised Jesus Christ from the dead. The Kingdom of GOD is a Spiritual Kingdom that is to have full dominion on the earth as in heaven. Romans 8:11 (English Standard Version - ESV) says,

If the same Spirit of Him who raised Jesus from the dead dwells in you, He who raised Christ Jesus from the dead will also give life to your mortal bodies through the Spirit who lives in you.

The Gospel of the Kingdom, as it is referred to in Matthew 24:14, is the message that we carry in earthen vessels to proclaim as a testimony to every nation.

Carrying the message of the Kingdom of GOD does not merely mean preaching the tenets of this gospel. It means to exemplify the message through how we live our lives and respond to daily encounters. As we go through life, many challenges will come to test the boundaries of what's in the heart. GOD communicates to and through our hearts His message of faith, hope, and love as with other attributes. I'm referring to the heart of GOD'S Spirit living within you. The core of all our beliefs is rooted in the heart. Thy word have I hid in my heart that I may not sin against thee. Romans 10:8-10 (New King James Version) says,

But what does it say? The word is near you, in your mouth, and in your heart (the word of faith we preach).

That if you confess with your mouth the Lord Jesus and believe in your heart that GOD has raised Him from the dead, you will be saved.

For with the heart, one believes unto righteousness, and with the mouth, confession is made unto salvation.

We not only believe from the heart, but we also love with our hearts. Jesus commanded us to love. When Jesus was asked by a lawyer, "What is the great commandment?"

Jesus said unto him, thou shalt love the Lord thy GOD with all thy heart and with all thy how an individual conducts themselves, it would become very difficult for others to develop trust and with all thy mind.

This is the first and greatest commandment.

And the second is like unto it. Thou shall love thy neighbor as thyself.

On these two commandments hang all the law and the prophets. (Matthew 22:37-40).

When we obey these two commandments, we demonstrate our love for Jesus Christ.

Proverbs 3:3-5 Indicates to us that our heart can trust in the Lord within its highest capacity. Therefore, our trust emanates from the heart as well. Trust must have time to develop. It is a characteristic that springs from consistent displays of integrity and truth. Whenever there is inconsistency in how an individual conducts themselves, it becomes very difficult for others to develop trust or belief in them. Since all men and women are naturally flawed individuals, it is more difficult for trust to be initiated over the short term. Based on this fact, belief does not always come instantaneously but is acquired in increments of time and experiences. In this hour, we must pray that the Lord gives us keen spiritual discernment to apply in our daily walk.

The Book of Jude instructs us to build ourselves up in our most holy faith, praying in the Holy Ghost. Those who are built up in their most holy faith have spiritual immunity to defend against the contamination of the soul. Through a growing knowledge of Jesus Christ, we avail ourselves of GOD'S word and His Spirit. Through prayer, supplication with thanksgiving, and daily fellowship, we grow into the very image of Jesus Christ. Whenever we spend undisturbed, quality time fellowshipping in the spirit, we become acquainted with our knowledge of how GOD thinks and feels. This knowledge is spiritually and not naturally discerned. We begin to dislike what He dislikes, love what he loves, believe, and act as He does. Why? Because we are becoming more intimately acquainted with the glory of His person and presence through the Holy Spirit. The Holy Spirit will teach and show us everything concerning our Father as we avail ourselves to Him.

Jesus Christ was first revealed as the Son of man. All the fullness of GOD'S person and ability forever abides within Him because He and GOD are One. In other words, GOD sent Himself in the form of a man. His name was called Emmanuel, which means, GOD with us on earth. (Matthew 1:23).

The initial followers who were called by Jesus were first referred to as disciples. They willingly left everything to follow Jesus as He demonstrated the love of His Father through preaching and performing exploits of healing. In Matthew 10:1-15, Jesus sent out the twelve apostles with the spiritual authority to drive out unclean spirits and to heal all kinds of diseases and sicknesses. Before sending them, Jesus instructed them not to go to the Gentiles or the Samaritans but to the lost sheep of the house of Israel. Further, Jesus commissioned them to:

Preach, saying the kingdom of GOD is at hand.

Heal the sick.

Cleanse the lepers.

Raise the dead.

Cast out, devils.

This was their very first assignment in which they tasted the experience of walking in their apostleship. When Jesus sent out the twelve to accomplish their designated assignment, they manifested the works of true apostles. As their Master Teacher and Lord had given to them, they were instructed to give freely. The apostles operated in some of the supernatural functions of their office and in the authority of their anointing for the first time. They were to only discover the full measure of their apostleship upon receiving the baptism of the Holy Spirit on the Day of Pentecost. (Acts 2:1-31). After returning from their first assignment, the apostles came away from their experiences so excited! Did Jesus join in with their gleeful celebration? No, He did not. As they had seen Him heal the sick and cast out unclean spirits, they were also given the power and authority to do the same. But Jesus refocused them in His reply, saying,

I saw Satan fall like lightning from heaven.

Dennis J. Perkins

I have given you authority to trample on snakes and scorpions and to overcome all the power of the enemy, nothing will harm you.

However, do not rejoice that the spirits submit to you, but rejoice that your names are written in heaven. (Luke 10:18-19).

A true apostle of Jesus Christ is hand-picked, chosen, and sent by Him. This standard still holds today. There is nowhere in scripture saying that the ministry gift of the apostle has ceased to exist. Ephesians 4:11 makes a sound reference to this. Therefore, Jesus is still appointing those ministry gifts by the Holy Spirit. This ministry gift and any of the other four mentioned are only commissioned and authorized by Jesus Christ, not by mere men.

The twelve did not walk in the fullness of their apostleship until they received power from on high when the Holy Ghost made His entrance into the earthly realm. Their prayer and one accord created a portal of perfect entry on that special day. This was upon the Day of Pentecost when they had a powerful, life-changing encounter with the Holy Ghost. They came into greater knowledge and power at the moment the Holy Ghost came to live within them.

The Apostle Paul experienced this on the day that he was struck by a blinding light and knocked off his donkey while on the way to Damascus to further persecute the followers of Jesus Christ. His heart's desires were changed by his encounter with the Lord. Saul, before he was referred to as Paul, was very zealous in his pursuit to stomp out the fiery flames of this new, fast-growing spiritual movement. Christianity, as it was being called, became a serious threat to the religious establishment of that era and time. His encounter with the Lord, and experiencing the infilling of the Holy Ghost created a great zeal in Paul to attain to the highest levels of this most intimate knowledge of Jesus Christ. Philippians 3:10-14 (Updated New American Standard Bible) says,

That I may know Him, and the power of His resurrection and the fellowship of His sufferings being conformed to His death.

So that I may attain to the resurrection from the dead.

Not that I have already obtained it or have already become perfect, but I press on so that I may lay hold of that for which also I was laid hold of by Christ Jesus.

Brethren, I do not regard myself as having laid hold of it yet; but one thing I do: forgetting what lies behind and reaching forward to what lies ahead.

I press on toward the goal for the prize of the upward call of GOD in Christ Jesus.

The weights and cares from the past are never allowed into your next level. Paul knew that it would be impossible for him to press forward in his upward call if he continued to hold on to what identified him with Saul, the old him. He knew that whatever his security used to abide in, was no longer what would sustain him in his newly found life in Jesus Christ. Now that he ceased living as Saul, he had taken hold of a life hidden in this new identity in Christ. He was now a representative of a glorious kingdom. When we surrender the old life for our new nature in Jesus Christ, the old things pass away. They are now gone, and a new life begins. We are to cast those cares upon Jesus, for He cares for us.

The Apostle Paul was not satisfied with falling into status quo Christianity. He wasn't just satisfied with his salvation. He desired that all men be saved. The result is that Paul had taken on the heart of His Father in heaven. He wanted to attain the highest level of what GOD called and appointed him to do.

This apostle never gave in to prideful ideals and other wrongful attitudes of entitlement. Instead, he humbled himself to GOD. The Holy Spirit assisted Paul in humbling his heart as he gave himself to prayer and fellowship with GOD. Humility is one of the keys to accelerating spiritual growth. We must always be mindful that we are unable to accomplish anything, especially that which pertains to life and godliness without acknowledging GOD'S grace. Grace will make its entrance into our lives when we understand that without the Lord, we can do nothing. Yes, grace enters our lives through humility and surrender to the Lord. GOD gives grace to the humble. Not everyone is humble. We live in a culture of self-sufficient, and independent thinkers who are proud of their accomplishments. We should have a healthy level of care and integrity in whatever efforts we set forth to accomplish. When we render our best efforts to do what is good and pleasing to ourselves, we should be equally willing to share the same measure of effort to support others. Why is this important? It is because relative to what some believe. All believers in our Lord should be willing to follow the example, regardless of our status in life, whether small or great. It was out of love that Jesus took on mere flesh and blood to be the sacrificial Lamb of GOD who redeems the whole world from sin.

Promotions Come from GOD

For promotion cometh neither from the east, nor from the west, nor from the south,

But GOD is the judge, He putteth down one, and setteth up another. (Psalm 75:6-7)

Therefore, submit to GOD. Resist the devil and he will flee from you.

Draw near to GOD and He will draw near to you. Cleanse your hands, you sinners, and purify your hearts, you double-minded.

Lament and mourn and weep! Let your laughter be turned to mourning and your joy to gloom.

Humble yourselves in the sight of the Lord, and He will lift you up. (James 4:7-10).

In modern terms, the word elevation can be described in many ways. We have heard the term used within the confines of the church to promote someone from a lower position to one of a higher level of responsibility or authority. The word itself constitutes a literal or figurative form of upward trajectory. People experience natural elevations in life. As we understand, promotions are a part of a reward system in both the spiritual and physical realms. People aspire to experience different types of promotions. We often utilize manmade systems of promotion. The educational system, entertainment (music, sports), government, business, and religion are some examples of the avenues that people can use to promote themselves. There could be major misconceptions when any of the above are pursued as a primary means to acquire status for elevating an individual to the next level. Not everyone seeks promotion in this regard, but they enter a particular field of study to fulfill a dream or desire for which they have a bent or talent. I am not attempting to make those comparisons, but instead, to provoke focus on what GOD is doing to advance you and me into our next level. Yes, there are levels of spiritual growth that we all are given opportunities to attain. The process of growth comes with many levels of challenge. There may be some fear and intimidation encountered within the experience, but the fear never comes from GOD. GOD is love. Love has no fear. So how, or why would GOD induce fear? Although He does test us, He also encourages and instructs us not to fear. He often inspires us to break through our limited ways of thinking to propel us to new levels and higher callings in Christ Jesus. In this hour, GOD is not merely asking us to come up higher in the ways that we often think and live our lives. He requires those who follow the leading of His Holy Spirit to faithfully trust and obey Him. Obedience and submission, in a modern sense, may take on the connotation of being negative or weak. This is not the truth, but a lying spirit sent to sway us from the path of humility. We know that godly humility always precedes honor. A true servant of GOD does not assume a false posture or make any demands to acquire honor. A True servant will always exercise their duties or function out of a heart that is surrendered to the Lord. Out of that condition of his heart, they are to execute their kingdom-oriented duties. In the Kingdom of GOD, there is no me first. The Lord's business should take precedence over our wants and desires. All things are then added to your well-being when you have the proper posture and attitude. Blessed are the pure in heart, for they shall see GOD. (Matthew 5:8). Blessed are the meek, for they shall inherit the earth. (Matthew 5:5). Both obedience and

98

submission are two of the key attributes utilized to activate GOD'S standards of preservation and promotion, first within the family.

The family can be primarily considered as one of many microcosms of the world. It remains the foundation from which all civilizations come from. As GOD'S standards are maintained within the purposes that He created a family for, there will be lasting generational benefits. Societies flourish when they have a makeup of morally strong families. When a man and woman become one in holy matrimony, it can be considered a natural elevation. Why? Because GOD ordained marriage. It is a mystery but is an earthly example of Jesus Christ as the head of His Church, which is called His Body. Children are called a heritage from the Lord. Blessed are those whose quiver is full of them. (Psalm 127:3-5).

In Ephesians 6:1, the scripture says,

Children, obey your parents in the LORD, for this is right. That it may go well with you and that you may enjoy a long life on the earth. Fathers do not exasperate your children; instead, bring them up in the training and instruction of the Lord.

Ephesians 5:22-25 says,

Wives, submit yourselves unto your own husbands as unto the Lord.

For the husband is the head of the wife, even as Christ is the head of the church, and He is the savior of the body.

Therefore, as the church is subject unto Christ, so let the wives be to their own husbands in everything.

Husbands, love your wives, even as Christ also loved the church, and gave Himself for it.

That he might sanctify and cleanse it with the washing of water by the word.

There is no wonder that GOD'S standard for marriage and family has been under such a constant barrage of malicious attacks, for not only decades but for centuries. When we lack understanding of the standards by which GOD uses to promote, the enemy will then take full advantage of our deficit of knowledge. He knows that when knowledge is suppressed or not given a primary place of importance, people become open prey for destruction. There are no shortcuts to promotion. This is why men pleasing, manipulating, or posturing themselves for positions of promotion will not work in GOD'S Kingdom. All leaders in the Kingdom of GOD should truly possess a purity of love and care for those they have been given responsibility and oversight.

In 1 Peter 5:2-7, The apostle admonishes, particularly elders, but it applies to all leaders within the established churches of that time to:

Shepherd the flock of GOD, which is among you, serving as overseers, not by compulsion, but willingly, not for dishonest gain, but eagerly,

Nor as being lords over those entrusted to you, but being examples to the flock when the Chief Shepherd appears, you will receive the crown of glory that does not fade away.

Therefore, humble yourselves under the mighty hand of GOD that He may exalt you in due time, casting all your care upon Him, for He cares for you.

Likewise, you younger people, submit yourselves to your elders. Yes, all of you be submissive to one another, and clothed with humility, for GOD resists the proud, but gives grace to the humble.

Are you Prepared for What Lies Ahead?

For mainly the last four years, the spiritually sensitive have witnessed such a heightened onslaught of the enemy's tactics being deployed to stifle or delay creativity and forward progress. One of the main reasons we've experienced a full-court press of the opposition with such frequency is that we are threatening his unseen barriers. Pressing toward the mark for the high calling of GOD calls for the implementation of heightened offensive attacks through prayer and intercession to break down the enemy's defensive barriers. Can we do this alone? No, in most cases, it takes a team to engage and overtake the enemy successfully. This is why we must be connected to GOD'S plan. GOD'S plan is truly implemented through our willingness to walk in oneness with His will. Can you imagine how much of a force we could be if we lived in unity with one another?

So many people use the word unity wrongfully. They use the term to falsely sway others to come alongside a selfishly motivated plan to further promote their carnal desires. Our unity in Jesus Christ is having the same Spirit that gives us resurrection power. That unity discerns, rightfully acknowledges, and encourages the valuable gifts in others. You don't have to compete with another person when what you offer is unique and different. The value in your gifts is meant to complement the unit that you are assigned to. When the love of GOD is at the center of our unity, we will experience far more successes than failures. Whatever shortcomings are discovered will be worked through more readily and easily. Then, the love that binds us together will not give us any place for failure because love never fails. When operating within the spirit of unity in Christ, we ignite the enforcements of heaven to back up every word that supports GOD'S will on earth. As we live in this reality, you and I willingly take it upon ourselves to be most mindful and clearer in understanding our proper position and individual roles. This is why the enemy works so hard to get us out of character. He does so with distractions, inordinate attachments, and other things designed to get us off the mark. We must know our position in Christ Jesus to complement one another better, assuring that every person functions at the height of their calling.

Since we are in a spiritual war, we must never forget to dress appropriately, having the whole armor of GOD on. How do you put on your clothes each day? Do you dress in public or privately? Putting on the whole armor of GOD is based upon your personal, intimate preparation. What you do in private develops your integrity. GOD sees all that we do, but even if by chance He couldn't see us, we must exercise faithfulness to the knowledge of His righteous cause and calling. Given our preparedness, as stated earlier, dress appropriately. Ephesians 6:13-18 (NKJV) clarifies this for us.

5. Stand, therefore, having girded your waist with truth.

6. Having put on the breastplate of righteousness.

7. Having shod your feet with the preparation of the gospel of peace.

8. Above all, take the shield of faith with which you will be able to quench all the fiery darts of the wicked one.

9. Take up the helmet of salvation and,

10. The sword of the Spirit, which is the word of GOD.

11. Praying always with all prayer and supplication in the Spirit, being watchful to this end with all perseverance and supplication for all the saints.

The Apostle Paul solicits that prayers also be made for him as well. Why? So that utterance be given to him, that he may open his mouth boldly to make known the mystery of the gospel. Paul knew his position and the calling that GOD had upon his life. So, he knew that he had to be mindful and focused on what he was charged to do. Was this pertaining just to his ministry? No, it was not for any selfish motivation of his own. It was for the forward progress and growth of the body of believers in Jesus Christ's gospel. We have to be ready and always prepared to fight the good fight of faith. Whether an individual is aware, or not, the enemy is fully engaged in an all-out spiritual war. In any legitimate war, there are many casualties. Throughout this entire period that I previously referred to, there have been so many battles, and they continue. GOD is speaking to those who have spiritual ears to hear and spiritual eyes to see. Our natural mind cannot understand or perceive what can only be discerned by the Holy Spirit. It is generally of a common belief that our misconceptions about serving GOD are traditionally rooted in multiple erred religious doctrines and beliefs. Whether intentional or not, they have contributed significantly to a severe, prolonged drought in the spiritual development of countless people. Religious, doctrinal teachings have led to a fragmented approach to people's reverence and daily walk with GOD. Many religious activities or belief systems have ultimately become a poor substitution for how we go about serving GOD, while it is faith alone that pleases Him. Neither does any work alone justify us. Whatever kind of work we do, we must do it in faith. Works of faith will never produce any idle or wasteful outcomes because there is no waste in GOD'S Kingdom. Works of faith will always produce helpful and consumable good fruit. We find in the scriptures that they shall live by their faith. Galatians 3:10-11 Updated New American Standard says,

For as many as are of the works of the Law are under a curse; for it is written, "Cursed is everyone who does not abide by all things written in the Book of the Law, to perform them.

Now that no one is justified by the Law before GOD is evident; for, the righteous man shall live by faith."

Hebrews 11:1says,

Now faith is the substance of things hoped for, the evidence of things not seen.

This would easily clarify the fact that our works alone do not save us, nor do they make us righteous. Ever since the word of GOD was spoken, or transcribed, there has been a competitive entity raised out of a spirit of jealousy to steal the sheep of the Lord from under the protective covering of ordained, anointed shepherds that truly love GOD'S way. GOD'S ways are absent of any control, through spiritual manipulation or condemnation. The spirit of religion has run rampant in a quest to replace the Spirit of the Lord. If there is little or no discernment imparted by the Holy Ghost, how can we tell if what is being experienced is from GOD? 1 John 4 NIV says,

Dear friends, do not believe every spirit but test the spirits to see whether they are from GOD because many false prophets have gone out into the world. But every spirit that does not acknowledge Jesus is not from GOD.

104

The word acknowledge carries a great deal of weight when applied to Proverbs 3:5-6 NIV.

Trust In the Lord with all your heart and lean not on your own understanding.

In all your ways acknowledge Him, and He will make your paths straight.

Otherwise, in all that you do, do it with the highest reverence and praise that can be offered to GOD as the Chief Authority in every aspect of your life. So proper acknowledgment means more than giving service with words but living it, even in the closest of quarters or in the most private and intimate situations when no one sees you except GOD.

The same spirit that prevailed in the Pharisees and the Sadducees' day has survived and is enforced even to this date. Many churches on the earth have taken on a model of a Pharisaical approach system. This system is regulated by doctrinal rules and laws that are void of the Holy Spirit. They preach a form of salvation that places a strong emphasis on good deeds, ethical works, and activities. The activities described are never to be compared with living an impactfully, surrendered life inside of the Law of Love.

In Matthew 22:37-40 Jesus replied,

Love the Lord your GOD with all your heart and with all your soul and with all your mind.

This is the first and greatest commandment.

And the second is like it: Love your neighbor as yourself.

All the Law and Prophets hang on these two commandments.

Jesus held the commandments to love in the absolute highest esteem, so much so that He equated them with obeying all of the Laws given to Moses.

Man-made practices have applied their religious interpretations to serving or pleasing God. They render worship a form of godliness that denies the power of the living God. Therefore, the devil uses religion to blind the eyes of those who think they see. Here is where the thief has come in to hoodwink and hijack the true, pure religion referred to in James 1:27. Let's look at the scripture in context.

James 1:25-27 says,

But one who looks intently at the perfect law of liberty and abides by it, not having become a forgetful hearer but an effectual doer, this man will be blessed in what he does.

If anyone thinks himself to be religious, and yet does not bridle his tongue but deceives his own heart, this man's religion is worthless.

Pure and undefiled religion in the sight of our GOD and Father is this: to visit orphans and widows in their distress and to keep oneself unstained by the world.

We must maintain an ongoing ability to be slow in our reactions, especially when it comes to frequently speaking. Keeping proper control over our conversation and use of words proves to be a very powerful thing. When we fail to exercise self-control over our tongue, we can easily enter a world of self-deception, reaching a point where we lose direction. See the book of James concerning the tongue.

This is one of the primary reasons that we find so much division, confusion, and individual, and corporate lack of intimacy with GOD. Rather than surrendering to the Lord Jesus Christ, the enemy gains an entrance through what looks or sounds like the real thing. What some religious institutions consider sound doctrine becomes indoctrination when it is mechanically implemented and maintained. This does not work to advance the Kingdom of GOD in any way. It limits spiritual development. This is the strategy that the devil has used for so long. We must be about the business of discerning the Spirit of GOD. The devil intends to skew our ability to discern the truth from the lie. True worship comes out of the heart but is induced and inspired by the spirit of GOD which lives in us. John 4:24 says,

GOD is Spirit, and they that worship Him must worship Him in spirit and in truth.

In Genesis 1:26, it is said that GOD made man in His image and likeness. So, GOD being a Spirit Himself, first made man a living soul, because he came from the earth. The Lord utilizes man as His portal to represent Him on earth. Therefore, man is composed of soul, body, and spirit. How would man worship the Lord in spirit and truth without being a spirit? Thus, the soul and body are not enough. We must connect with our spirit as it relates, communicates, and gives service to GOD, the Father of spirits.

Hebrews 12:9 (NIV) says,

Moreover, we have all had human fathers who disciplined us, and we respected them for it. How much more should we submit to the Father of spirits and live?

Since we live by the Spirit, let us also keep in step with the Spirit. (Galatians 5:25 NIV).

The Spirit of the LORD is doing something new in this hour. When referring to "this hour," I am emphasizing what is present-day or in the current events that we're now experiencing. There is always a set time for everything that GOD does. Therefore, we must understand that the set times are always of His choosing, and not ours. I am emphasizing this because so many of us are currently waiting for the manifestation of a promise being fulfilled by the Lord. Some of us have waited for years, while others have far less. Unfortunately, we sometimes question whether we have heard from the Lord. GOD'S process of elevation is far different from our concepts of what it truly means. Why? His prerequisites are entirely based upon His weights and standards within a person's heart. GOD knows that every work of man proceeds from within the heart. When a person's heart is yielded, He can then work with that individual to further enhance the qualities and abilities necessary to carry out His assignment. Unlike the world, promotion is not determined by what you know intellectually and who you know socially or even politically. We must find a distinct place of living in heartfelt surrender while having a working knowledge of GOD'S will. To the average on-looker who does not exercise spiritual discernment, GOD'S process can seem unfair, or even nonexistent. On the other hand, some stand on a firm foundation of faith, knowing the will of GOD for their life. Their belief establishes them in a faith and hope that are not easily moved or shaken. As they live through each experience, they develop a track record that withstands the storms of life, because they know Who stands with them. We are to never cease in our efforts to grow up in spiritual things. GOD wants us to not only be salt and light. He wants us to be fruitful and very mature in spiritual character as well. Speaking of being productive, we're not merely bearing fruit for it to be seen, but to add flavor and sustenance to the lives of others (especially those in the Body of Christ). GOD will move upon those

108

whom He chooses, to fulfill His excellent work, but there is always a waiting process. From its inception until its fulfillment, God has an appointed time set aside to promote those who withstand each test. Promotion doesn't come in some of the traditional ways that you or I would typically think. It is unlike anything that anyone has experienced in their lifetime. GOD is very serious and laser-focused on fulfilling His plans and purposes regarding His Kingdom. Those who are called and chosen by Him should first come to the knowledge that the Kingdom of GOD dwells within them. Luke 17:20-21 says,

And when He was demanded of the Pharisees, when the Kingdom of God should come, He answered them and said, The Kingdom of GOD cometh not with observation.

Neither shall they say, Lo here! Or, lo there! For behold, the Kingdom of GOD is within you.

Finding your rightful place and positioning is a journey of greater heights and depths. The Holy Spirit is our Advocate, but we must pursue a relationship with Him to get to know Christ's mind. We can live in the Spirit, move in the Spirit, and experience great joy and fulfillment as we look to God for sustenance.

When GOD created the heavens and the earth by His word, the process of evolution and expansion of the galaxies began. His spoken words have not changed in either creative ability or power. For countless centuries, all of creation has continuously experienced evolutionary cycles. It has always been GOD'S plan to have synergy within the makeup of all things created by Him. All things work together in a complimentary manner. Whether we experience favorable or unfavorable situations, they can be used for our good. They normally expose the inadequate qualities we bear within us. Speaking of exposure; we are living in appointed times. These times require the enforcement of truth to shine as a light upon all the hidden works of darkness. The things that have been whispered behind closed doors, in the most secret places, are now being exposed to the world. Therefore, evil will have no hiding place.

The hidden things of darkness are being revealed in the mountain of religion. There are those in ministry who may have started with pure intentions to espouse the gospel of Jesus Christ, but upon receiving a measure of notoriety, influence, and what the world deems as success, they experienced a change in their motives of operation. Once that takes place, the spirit of pride stepped in to serve as an unholy portal for all manner of sin to creep into the church. The enemy has used this tactic on a grand scale to bring demise and confusion, to, in essence, recreate the scenario that took place in the Garden of Eden that concerned the tree of the knowledge of good and evil. The tree itself was not evil, but the very act of treasonous disobedience contaminated man, opening their eyes to the realm of viewing, feeling, and perceiving things through the flesh, and not by the spirit.

I believe that GOD is speaking directly to those open to hearing His voice. Another way that He often speaks to us is through dreams and visions. When He releases anyone to share a dream, it should contain a message that, when shared, will resonate with the hearer (the one who hears with spiritual ears). Dreams can prophesy things to come. They give messages that go far beyond our understanding. They warn of impending danger and give encouragement and instructions for navigating situations that we are currently engaged in, or those things that are forthcoming.

The Elevator Dream (Representing GOD'S Elevation)

Dreams and visions are meant by GOD to speak to something that is occurring or to give us a glimpse of what is to come. I don't always think that every dream God gives me is a message exclusive to me. It could involve many people whose life situations resonate with the overriding messages contained in the dream.

In early January of 2024, I had a dream which consisted of two scenarios. The first was of me visiting someone in a hospital room. I saw myself quietly sitting there on a couch to provide some level of comfort and support to the patient. The scene quickly shifted to what appeared to be a series of elevators located adjacent to the grand lobby of a luxury hotel. As I stood waiting among many others, anticipating the arrival of the elevators to take me to my designated floor, a beautiful young lady recognized me. Even though she was of a younger adult age, her expressions were purely innocent and childlike. She never spoke to me but appeared to be extremely overjoyed to see me. Her joyfulness was contagious, as it generated a smile from me towards her. Three women were standing to my right, and they became increasingly annoyed with her unabated giddiness. They spoke negatively, but the young lady's joy was undisturbed. I continued to smile as I witnessed the pure and innocent glow on her face. This was where my dream ended.

Preparation for Elevation

This dream was very vivid and impactful. It grew in relevance because the images kept playing over and over in my mind. They have never left me. It was not until later that week, while in intercessory prayer, that the Holy Spirit brought a vision of the elevators back to me. I felt the unction to speak what I was envisioning. I only saw a series of closed elevators. Then I began to speak and heard, "This is GOD'S time to elevate His people. Many people will be ready to step into this new era through their preparation and continued intimacy with GOD. Those who are prepared will go through a period of waiting, but throughout the entire time of their waiting, they do so with a high level of joyful anticipation. Within the anticipation lies an expectation of what is to be implemented. I can feel the excitement arising even as I write these words. This level of expectation leads to a joyful anticipation of what is to come. Some will not ascend, because of their lack of preparedness and lack of intimacy with the Lord. This is something that will happen imminently, and it will happen very soon. It will catch many people off guard, so some people will literally be left out, or left behind. This could be described as a type of rapture because GOD chose this specific time to elevate His people with spiritual enlightenment, and even in reverential regard, meaning having a proper fear of the Lord. We are coming into a richer knowledge of not only who GOD is, but also, what we mean to Him. We will come into a greater knowledge and be able to fully express the truth of our divine nature on earth as in heaven. Those individuals that are disinterested and uncommitted will be left out. They will not receive due to their lack of readiness and improper alignment or positioning with the Lord and His people. This event will be so subtle that it will go unnoticed by the world. Those of us who incline our ears to hear what GOD is speaking, see what He is revealing, and readily apply the faith in what is revealed with corresponding action; will activate the Kingdom of GOD in this realm.

We must be prepared for the work that lies ahead. Therefore, now is the time to be steadfast, always on the alert and in a posture of readiness. We must be mindful to surround ourselves with others who know what the will of the Lord is for this hour. Not only are they to be sound in their living knowledge of the word of GOD, but also in their lifestyle; showing the fruit of the Spirit of life that is in Christ Jesus.

Matthew 25:1-13 NKJV

Then the kingdom of heaven shall be likened to ten virgins who took their lamps and went out to meet the bridegroom.

Now five of them were wise, and five were foolish.

Those who were foolish took their lamps and took no oil with them.

But the wise took oil in their vessels with their lamps.

But while the bridegroom was delayed, they all slumbered and slept.

And at midnight a cry was heard; Behold, the bridegroom is coming, go out to meet him!

Then all those virgins arose and trimmed their lamps.

And the foolish said to the wise, "Give us some of your oil, for our lamps are going out.

But the wise answered saying, No, lest there should not be enough for us and you; but go rather to those who sell, and buy for yourselves.

And while they went to buy, the bridegroom came, and those who were ready went in with him to the wedding, and the door was shut.

Afterward, the other virgins came also, saying "Lord, Lord, open to us!"

But He answered and said, "Assuredly, I say to you, I do not know you.

Watch, therefore, for you know neither the day nor the hour in which the Son of Man is coming".

Why weren't the five foolish virgins able to enter the shut door upon demanding entrance? It was because they were not adequately prepared. They were not present upon the bridegroom's arrival, nor did they have the required oil. Their lamps were not filled enough to support their journey as they waited for the bridegroom to arrive. This symbolizes the importance of having intimate knowledge of the Lord through His words, prayers, praise, and listening to Him. Without having the level of intimacy that the Lord requires, there was no relationship. Did you notice how significant the oil was? The oil is representative of the anointing of the Lord. It does not randomly show up unless the authorization of the Spirit of GOD gives it. Various types of anointings come upon people to confirm the residence and impartation of a gift or a calling by the Spirit of GOD. Anointings come from GOD with specific purposes. All anointings are not the same but vary according to the magnitude of the need. In Luke 4:18-19, Jesus said,

The Spirit of the Lord is upon Me because He has anointed Me to preach the gospel to the poor. He has sent Me to heal the brokenhearted. To proclaim liberty to the captives, and recovery of sight to the blind. To set at liberty those who are oppressed.

To proclaim the acceptable year of the Lord.

If you are filled with the Spirit of GOD, then you have His anointing within you. Therefore, that anointing comes with specific gifts and a calling as well. Many people live their entire lives under repressive influences that work to suppress these very gifts that GOD gave to be used for the benefit of others.

116

Gifts are meant to be given away. Callings have to do with our specific assignments that the Lord gives to fulfill His purposes. Your spiritual and natural gifts will, in turn, make room for you and bring you before the right people, places, and things that the Lord has ordained.

Saul was the first anointed King or Prince of Israel. He possessed all the desirable physical traits that would please his future subjects. Over a brief period, Saul proved to be a mighty man of war in defense of his people. He was also self-willed and not as reverent towards the word of the Lord, which was spoken through Samuel. Over time, the Lord grew increasingly displeased with King Saul's dishonorable acts of disobedience, which showed his lack of proper reverence for the Lord. Therefore, King Saul was stripped of the spiritual anointing specifically given to rule God's people. Upon this occurrence, GOD led Samuel to the house of Jesse to find Saul's replacement as king. Samuel initially thought that GOD would use a similar protocol as when He selected Saul. Saul was very handsome and tall, which made him unique to most men. The Lord spoke to Samuel before he met with Saul, saying that the next day, a man would come out of the tribe of Benjamin. He instructed the prophet that this man would be anointed king over His people. GOD makes no mistakes. He knew in advance the content of Saul's character and heart. It was unclear what other characteristics the Lord sought to qualify him as a candidate. The Lord did not transfer the man, Saul's anointing. It was the anointing that the Lord gave specifically to kings and rulers over select nations of people. The anointing is always given to advance GOD'S purposes. Isaiah 10:24-27 KJV lends us more insight on this.

Therefore, thus says the Lord GOD of hosts, O my people that dwell in Zion, do not be afraid of the Assyrian. He shall strike you with a rod, and lift up his staff against you, in the manner of Egypt.

For yet a very little while and the indignation will cease as will My anger in their destruction.

And the Lord of hosts shall stir up a scourge for him according to the slaughter of Midian at the rock of Oreb, as His rod was on the sea so will He lift it in the manner of Egypt.

And it shall come to pass in that day that his burden will be taken away from your shoulder. And the yoke from your neck. And the yoke will be destroyed because of the anointing oil.

Through the anointing oil, GOD used Samuel to perform this powerful act that set David apart to lead His people. The power and favor of GOD were heavily on David for many years before his official crowning as king. Although David was not perfect in all his ways, his heart towards GOD permitted great anointings to emerge and persist throughout each stage of his entire public life: 1) as a psalmist and minstrel, characteristic of the prophetic anointing. 2) as a giant slayer and warrior, and 3) as King over the twelve tribes of Israel.

With the anointing of GOD, you possess the exact things that will address questions and provide sustenance wherever there is a specific need. Your contributions will assist others with their advancement to higher levels. Will you invest with that gift that GOD placed within you? How do you think GOD sees this? Let's look at the following parable in Matthew 25:14-18.

For the kingdom of heaven is as a man traveling into a far country, who called his own servants, and delivered unto them his goods.

Dennis J. Perkins

And unto one he gave five talents, to another two, and to another one; to every man according to his several ability, and straightway took his journey.

Then he that had received the five talents went and traded with the same and made them other five talents.

And likewise, he that had received two, he also gained other two.

But he that had received one went and digged in the earth, and hid his lord's money.

This parable is not strictly about what, or how much GOD will place in our charge. It is about being faithful to whatever amount. It also denotes the responsibility that should be taken with whatever the Lord entrusts into our hands for His purposes. Note that these three people were servants of an employer who expected them to deliver a service that would result in a profitable gain. The employer knew their abilities, which entailed their weaknesses and strengths. This is a beautiful example of how GOD sees and knows the level of the skills imparted to us. As you can see, GOD is the source of all provision for His divine purposes. He never squanders any resources that are within His authority to discharge. GOD is most generous and gives us more abundantly, but He is not a waster. Let us be committed and dedicated to our service to Him, always striving to be faithful and responsible in all we do.

The servant that received the one talent immediately went and buried it to hide the lord's money. The other two servants took their money, made investments, and each doubled what was given to them. The Lord despises irresponsibility and laziness. He accounts for this by being wicked and slothful. We must not be so fearful in taking on the responsibility the Lord gives us. Stay very prayerful about everything that comes into your hands, recognizing that every perfect gift comes from above.

It comes from the Father of lights, for whom there is neither variableness nor shadow of changing. (James 1:17-18). GOD is the greatest of all tacticians. He is precise in all his calculations; He never wavers or mistakenly gives any assignment with less than what we need to complete any task. The voice of fear speaks from a very different narrative. Listening to a voice foreign to the Lord's words will create doubt and fearfulness in carrying out the assignment. I will repeat this. The talents represent a specific responsibility that GOD gives according to our ability. We must not fail to understand that GOD will not give us more than what is in our ability to accomplish. If we are content with what we have and faithfully work within the boundaries of those resources, whether large or small, GOD will entrust us with more. Why? It is because He takes joy in our growth and increase.

I pray that the Lord causes more significant increases for you and your family. May you have an abundance for every good work that He assigns you. I speak GOD'S increase and favor over your life. The blessing of the Lord will always make you rich, and it will not add any intended anxiety or sorrow. May He bless you more and more, you and your children, and your children's children. I keep hearing: "Stay within your assignment." It is important to 1) know your role in the broader scope of the Kingdom of GOD, 2) the proper timing, and 3) the location for each assignment. We must pray and seek the Lord's continual guidance in our endeavors. I will repeat this again and again. GOD assigns nothing without giving us the capacity to complete the work. He will give us the means and materials we need to implement the assignment and the wisdom, knowledge, and understanding to complete the task at hand.

The people with a kingdom mindset will present the same characteristics as those of the children of Issachar. The children of Issachar knew the importance and urgency of the times they lived in but were also given the prophetic mandate and the knowledge to carry out the vision. (1 Chronicles 12:32). We, too, must be about our Father's business in carrying forth His righteousness, justice, and the word of truth. When we consistently work out our salvation as we revere the Lord, the Kingdom of GOD populates the earth with the light and riches of His glory. The glory of the Lord must arise in you and me to fulfill the business of our Father in heaven. 1 Corinthians 4:6-7 says,

For it is the GOD who commanded the light to shine out of darkness, who has shone in our hearts to give the light of the knowledge of the glory of GOD in the face of Jesus Christ.

Serving the Lord's Body in the Spirit of Humility

In the early days of the church, some apostles and teachers were highly acclaimed among the members of the Body of Christ. This caused elements of disunity, which the Apostle Paul strongly addressed then, and we must do so as well. Paul spoke about this in 1 Corinthians 3:1-4. We must remember that our unity in the Body of Christ is crucial. It binds us together and makes us a strong, supportive community.

And I, brethren, could not speak to you as to spiritual people but as to carnal, as to babes in Christ.

I fed you with milk and not with solid food; until now you were not able to receive it, and even now you are still not able.

For you are still carnal. For where there are envy, strife, and divisions among you, are you not carnal and behaving like mere men?

As we've learned, the church has been severely divided and more fragmented. GOD is raising a standard against principalities and powers that have come against the advancement of the true church. I'm referring to the church that Jesus spoke of in Matthew 16:18. It has never been GOD'S intention to allow the remnant Body of Christ to fail, but to prevail against every spiritual onslaught. There is a great purging to correct the injustices committed to bring demise and confusion. Some purposely spy on the true liberty only the Holy Spirit can give. They also attempt to subvert that freedom and turn the freedom into bondage. They usurp the Spirit of

GOD to subdue it by enforcing doctrines that are false, orchestrated, and controlled by the flesh. GOD is bringing the Sword of His Spirit to divide the word of truth rightly. There is no guesswork in the Lord. He will make everything plain and understandable when we allow the Holy Spirit back into our lives and the church. He is separating what is soulish from what is the Spirit of Truth.

Galatians 2:4-5 NIV says,

This matter arose because some false believers had infiltrated our ranks to spy on the freedom we have in Christ Jesus and to enslave us.

We did not give in to them for a moment so that the gospel's truth might be preserved for you.

So, we have had two churches simultaneously in operation: 1) a carnally inspired church governed by the works of the flesh, and 2) a remnant church that the Holy Spirit of GOD leads. This duality is more than unhealthy but truly leaves an opportunity for the enemy to do irreparable damage to those easily carried away by his deception. There are those at high levels who work in concert with the devil to create spiritual interferences designed to disrupt and, if possible, destroy any aspect of unity. The devil knows that the blessing of the Lord abides more fervently, where the spirit of unity is unabated, and freedom is allowed. Psalm 133 KJV expresses the beauty and power found in the true spirit of unity. It is so eloquently described in the words of David's beautiful psalm.

Consider the beauty and joy that comes from brethren dwelling together in unity. It is a sight to behold, a testament to the power of love and the grace of our Lord.

It is like the precious ointment upon the head, that ran down upon the beard even Aaron's beard that went down to the skirts of his garments.

As the dew of Hermon, and as the dew that descended upon the mountains of Zion: for there the Lord commanded the blessing, even life for evermore.

Love is the cornerstone of unity. To truly experience the fullness of unity, we must walk in love towards one another. It is not just a commandment but a necessity for our spiritual growth and the health of the Body of Christ.

We must be aware of our roles and assignments and know the proper timing of our commitment.

There is an extreme need for the Body of Christ to be properly led by the Holy Spirit. We have ground forces that I would equate with officers in the military forces of the Kingdom of GOD. The Holy Spirit is duly assigned to give directions to the ground forces that take their instructions from those enlisted as apostles, prophets, evangelists, pastors, and teachers. They are tasked with ensuring that the body, in its entirety, comes into the unity of faith and the knowledge of the Son of GOD in all maturity until we exhibit the very image and fullness of Jesus Christ. (Ephesians 4:13). We have sometimes suffered many unnecessary casualties and injuries due to impure motivations and the ill-preparedness of self-appointed ministers of the gospel. On top of this, the majority of the church's members have contributed to the furtherance of its demise. Many believe someone else is responsible for their spiritual growth and maturity. As stated earlier in Ephesians 4:13, the five levels of ministry gifts are to carry the anointing and function in their roles. The people must understand that codependence upon men is not the way to accomplish what GOD desires. Each ministry gift carries its distinct anointing and mantle to impart to those who hunger and thirst for righteousness. I am referring to the righteousness of GOD that is in Christ Jesus. We are to value the ministry and spiritual gifts of the Lord. They are to be given proper respect and honor as men/women of GOD. Just remember that GOD is a jealous GOD. He will not put up with idolatry of any kind. Get into His word, seek His presence, speak to Him, hear His voice, and obey. You and I have been given the same access to the Holy Spirit, who deeply cares about our spiritual development.

What are You Willing to Sacrifice?

There comes a time when we may be required to give up some creature comforts or something of far greater significance. To the individual involved in making a notable sacrifice, it will not usually prove to be comparable with what they chose to leave behind. Believers are to go through tests and trials to establish and increase their level of faith. As they increase in faith, they also grow in their ability to please the Lord. Sacrifice derives from a heartfelt surrender of all of your gifts and even your plans to the Lord. Giving sacrificially is not a form of heroism but is a work that aligns and connects with the efforts of others. This produces a synergistic flow of the spirit to create a symphony of one living sound that vibrationally elevates people to new service levels. Abraham was a man of GOD whom we know as the Father of Faith. He was willing to make sacrifices by leaving the comforts of his father's house and the familiar surroundings of his native country. The Lord greatly honors the sacrifices that Abraham and those like him were willing to make. They set a standard for those who would come after them. These men and women are our examples. I know people who willfully sacrifice everything in their dedication and service to the Lord. What inspires these individuals is their love for the Lord and His people. As much as sacrificial service means to GOD, obedience is the motivating factor that activates His rewards. (Deuteronomy 11:26-28). Obedience is the key that unlocks God's rewards, and it should be the guiding principle in our spiritual journey.

1 Samuel 15:22 KJV says,

Behold, to obey is better than sacrifice, and to hearken than the fat of rams.

When looking at the life of Abraham, you see a consistent thread of situations that detail his acts of obedience to the Lord. His willingness to obey the Lord led him to possess lands as the Lord further enlarged his territories. He also acquired an unfathomable inheritance, which he would never have experienced without his obedience. Abraham (even when called Abram) was consistently single-minded and focused on every effort to do all GOD told him. Abraham knew that the Lord was sovereign and that He could be trusted entirely. Therefore, his faith was readily activated by the words GOD spoke. Faith was received in the heart of Abraham as he attentively listened to the word of the Lord. (Romans 10:17). He took corresponding action based on his belief in GOD. He did so regardless of the consequence, the cost, or the outcome.

Romans 4:1-5 KJV says,

For if Abraham were justified by works, he hath whereof to glory, but not before GOD.

For what saith the scripture? Abraham believed GOD and it was counted unto him for righteousness.

Now to him that worketh is the reward not reckoned of grace, but of debt.

But to him that worketh not, but believeth on Him that justifieth the ungodly, his faith is counted for righteousness.

Abraham was so faithful that GOD could always depend on him to follow His instructions, no matter the situation. Yes, Abraham was tested in his faith, in his patience, and in his willingness to sacrificially give, even when that which was the most precious to him was required, his son of promise.

In Genesis 18, Abraham was standing at the tent door in the heat of that day. When he lifted his eyes and looked, three men were standing opposite of him. When he saw them, he immediately ran to meet them, bowed to the earth, and said, "My Lord, if now I have found favor in Your sight, please do not pass Your servant by." These were not angels, nor mere men. An angel would not have allowed any man to bow in honor to them because they know their status in the Lord's Kingdom well. They know well that GOD has appointed them to be the servants of men. Another indicator is found in verse 1 of chapter 18 (Updated New American Standard), saying,

"Now the Lord appeared to him by the oaks of Mamre, while he was sitting at the tent door in the heat of the day."

Abraham also referred to the one *whom he spoke with as Lord.* He was so privileged and honored by their presence that he hurriedly involved his entire household in showing them hospitality. Then, they said to him, "Where is Sarah your wife?" Abraham said that she was there in the tent. He said, "I will surely return to you at this time next year, and behold, Sarah, your wife will have a son." Sarah was standing there listening to what was said at the tent door. She laughed at the hearing of the word of GOD. Therefore, one year from that time, the son of her old age was conceived by faith, and given the name Isaac. Isaac in Hebrew means laughter. Is anything too difficult for the Lord? (Genesis 18:14).

Isaac was the son of GOD'S promise to them. Abraham waited for years to receive this cherished promise of a man-child that would be the beginning of generations to come. Although Hagar, Sarah's handmaiden, had borne a son, Ishmael, on her behalf, he was only a substitution for what GOD truly intended. He was not the son of promise but was born from an act of the flesh. Works of the flesh can never duplicate what the spirit of faith can. How many times do we receive a word from the Lord and make every effort to trust in the works of our own hands? We look to ourselves to manufacture what should have been conceived and birthed in the faith that comes from the word of GOD. Will what we build upon be able to stand? Not at all, unless we surrender everything to the Lord. It is never too late to repent and change course. It won't be perfect, but it can still be rectified. Remember, there is nothing too hard for GOD.

Abraham was willing to sacrifice whatever it took to please the Lord. GOD spoke to Abraham in Genesis 22:1- 15

Now it came to pass after these things that GOD tested Abraham! And He said, "Here I am."

Then He said, "Take now your son, your only son Isaac, whom you love, and go to the land of Moriah, and offer him there as a burnt offering on one of the mountains of which I shall tell you."

So, Abraham rose early in the morning, saddled his donkey, and took two of his young men with him and his son Isaac. He cut the wood for the burnt offering and rose and went to the place that GOD had told him.

On the third day, Abraham lifted his eyes and saw the place from afar.

Then Abraham said to his young men, "Stay here with the donkey, I and the boy will go over there and worship and come again to you.

And Abraham took the wood of the burnt offering and laid it on Isaac, his son. And he took in his hand the fire and knife. So, they went to both of them together.

And Isaac said to his father Abraham, "My father" And he said, "Here I am my son." He said, "Behold, the fire, and the wood, but where is the lamb for the burnt offering?"

And Abraham said, "My son, GOD will provide for himself the lamb for a burnt offering, my son," So they went both of them together.

Then they came to the place of which GOD had told him. And Abraham built an altar there and placed the wood in order, and he bound Isaac his son and laid him on the altar there and placed the wood in order, and he bound Isaac his son and laid him on the altar, upon the wood.

And Abraham stretched out his hand and took the knife to slay his son.

But the Angel of the Lord called to him from heaven and said, "Here I am."

And He said, "Do not lay your hand on the lad, or do anything to him; for now, I know that you fear GOD since you have not withheld your son, your only son, from Me."

Then Abraham lifted his eyes and looked, and there behind him was a ram caught in a thicket by its horns. So, Abraham went and took the ram, and offered it up for a burnt offering instead of his son.

And Abraham called the name of the place, The Lord Will Provide; as it is said to this day, "in the Mount of the Lord it shall be provided."

Because Abraham did not withhold his only son from the Lord, the Lord blessed and multiplied him and his descendants.

Jesus had an interesting conversation with a rich ruler who approached Him and asked, "What must I do to inherit eternal life?" This was the most important question, which required the greatest of all answers. Why? Because the answer provided the way, the truth, and the life for then, now, and always. Jesus said in Luke 18:20,

You know the commandments:

Do not commit adultery.

Do not murder.

Do not steal.

Do not bear false witness.

Honor your father and mother.

The rich ruler replied by saying, *"All these things I have kept from my youth."*

When Jesus heard this, He said to him, "One thing you still lack. Sell all that you have and distribute to the poor, and you will have treasure in heaven; and come, follow me."

But when he heard these things, he became very sad, for he was extremely rich.

Jesus seeing that he become sad, said, "How difficult it is for those who have wealth to enter the Kingdom of GOD."

Those who heard it said, "Then who can be saved?"

But he said, "What is impossible with man is possible with GOD."

And Peter said, "See, we have left our homes and followed you."

And he said to them, "Truly, I say to you, there is no one who has left house or wife or brothers or parents or children, for the sake of the Kingdom of GOD

Who will not receive many times more in this time, and in the age to come eternal life." (Luke 18:20-30 ESV).

The rich ruler could not part with his great wealth for one moment, for he found his identity in the wealth that he possessed. He could not at that time comprehend the abundance of the riches that the glory of GOD would provide because his trust abided in earthly possessions. When we are called and enlisted into service in the Lord's militia, we cannot afford to be consumed with the things that the world has to offer. He refused the elevation presented to him by the Master

Teacher, Jesus Christ. Jesus knew the location of this man's heart. He thought that because he had religiously dotted all of the "I's" and crossed every "T," he was secure in GOD. But Jesus exposed the true intentions of his heart. He divided what was soulish from what was the life of the spirit. There are balances in each of our lives that weigh what is of the soul and what measure of the spirit we walk in. The question should be asked, "What do you need most to sustain you?" I believe King Solomon had the proper perspective when he asked GOD to give him wisdom to govern His people. To be truly successful in any pursuit in life, we desperately need the knowledge of GOD.

The Principle Thing: Wisdom

Wisdom is not something that is reserved just for the privileged few. Wisdom comes from GOD and is given to anyone who sincerely asks for it. (James 1:5).

The Lord will not take back or repent of the wisdom He gives, even if it is not utilized. Some things have been freely given to us, and we sometimes need help activating them properly. What good is it to have wisdom that you fail to apply? If anyone devalues the knowledge freely made available by the Lord, their failure to activate wisdom will negatively and severely impact them. Proverbs 4:13 NIV says,

Hold on to instruction; do not let it go; guard it well, for it is your life.

Those of us who fail to understand the intrinsic value of wisdom do not have the revelation of its ability and power to preserve our lives. Did you know that wisdom was present with GOD during creation? Yes, wisdom, understanding, and knowledge were pivotal in formulating all things created, both on earth and in heaven. I would consider them the three-pronged impression that GOD left on all He made. (Proverbs 3:19-20). (See Proverbs 8).

1 Corinthians 1:28-31 says,

And the base things of the world and the things which are despised, GOD has chosen, and the things which are not, to bring to nothing the things that are,

That no flesh should glory in His presence.

Preparation for Elevation

But of Him, you are in Christ Jesus, who became wisdom from GOD and righteousness and sanctification and redemption for us.

As it is written, "He who glories, let him glory in the Lord."

Those who walk in the five primary ministry gifts mentioned in Ephesians 4:11 have a spiritual obligation to Jesus Christ to yield to the Holy Spirit to carry out and finish the work that He began. These gifts (apostles, prophets, evangelists, pastors, and teachers) are sacred to GOD and should never be taken lightly by those appointed to serve in these capacities. Don't people know that so many lives depend on the purity and power of what has been entrusted to them? Their lives are to be a demonstration of what Jesus Christ alone ordains. Therefore, proper, personal groundwork should be done within the hearts and minds of those administering these foundational gifts. Each ministry gift and individual calling must be appropriately appropriated. No one gets the privilege to lord over or take advantage of GOD'S royal, priestly inheritance. (1 Peter 2:9; 1 Peter 5:3). Jesus said that he who is greatest among you shall be your servant. Sound buildings are built upon firm, not so easily shaken foundations. The five ministry gifts are the foundation of the house built up in Christ Jesus and led by the power of the Holy Spirit.

In summation, with greater regularity, you will discern the fruit of those who have been duly prepared for elevation. (Proverbs 4:8; 1 Peter 5:6). They highly prize wisdom and have also divested themselves of pride, entitlement, and self-exaltation by walking in true humility. Anyone who does these things is proven and ready to exhibit their complete preparation for elevation.

A Prayer for Eternal Salvation

Father in heaven,

I come to You as a sinner who needs forgiveness. I believe that Jesus Christ died for my sins and that You raised Him from the dead. He conquered sin and death for me to have eternal life. I also believe that He is now seated at your right hand, making intercession for me.

Lord, I want You to know that I am sorry for the sins that I have committed. Please forgive me and cleanse my heart so I can freely serve You. Therefore, I surrender my life to You. Please help me to present my life as a living sacrifice, holy and acceptable to You as my reasonable service and worship.

I give You all the honor and praise as I ask these things in Jesus' name. Amen.

About the Author

Dennis James Perkins is a native of Yazoo City, Mississippi. After graduating from Yazoo City High School, he attended Jackson State University, where he joined the Sonic Boom of the South Marching Band.

After completing an undergraduate degree in business administration, Dennis later pursued his master's degree in community and agency counseling.

Throughout his adult life, he has primarily worked directly in the areas involving children and youth ages three to seventeen. As the years progressed, these experiences led to statewide positions, which gave him oversight of various programs that assisted families and vulnerable youth in the court systems serving all eighty-two counties of the State of Mississippi.

It was years before he discovered a closer walk with the Lord. Upon meeting Deborah N. Perkins (2018), his wife of twenty-eight years, a whirlwind of change took place in his life. This led him to acknowledge his spiritual calling into the ministry of the gospel of Jesus Christ. Through years of surrendered service in numerous capacities within the church, Dennis continues to grow in his capacity to express GOD'S love to and for His people. He currently lives in Brandon, Mississippi.

9 798894 804071